Sustained Shared Thin
in the Early ...

Used as a measure of quality in the ground-breaking Effective Provision of Pre-School Education (EPPE) project, Sustained Shared Thinking is fundamental to good early years practice. It costs nothing, yet research has shown that it improves outcomes for children by supporting their holistic development. This book clearly explains what Sustained Shared Thinking is and examines the skills and expertise needed to initiate, encourage and facilitate it.

The book explores the attitudes, knowledge and understanding that a practitioner must adopt in order to start or develop successful Sustained Shared Thinking. Combining theory with practical guidance, it demonstrates how it can be achieved, covering all aspects of early years practice including the Characteristics of Effective Learning, the Prime and Specific Areas of learning and development, the role of the practitioner, the environment and working with parents.

Features include:

- boxed links to key theory and research;
- practical strategies highlighted in the text;
- consideration of children at different ages and stages of development;
- links throughout to the Early Years Foundation Stage.

Written by a leading consultant who regularly delivers training on Sustained Shared Thinking, this will be an essential text for students on foundation degree and childhood studies courses as well as early years practitioners.

Kathy Brodie is an Early Years Consultant and Lecturer in Childhood Studies at Stockport College, UK. She delivers training on planning, observations, schema, working with under 2s, outdoor play, Sustained Shared Thinking, the EYFS and Sparkly Thinking.

Sustained Shared Thinking

in the Early Years

Linking theory to practice

Kathy Brodie

Routledge
Taylor & Francis Group

LONDON AND NEW YORK

First published 2014
by Routledge
2 Park Square, Milton Park, Abingdon, Oxon OX14 4RN

and by Routledge
711 Third Avenue, New York, NY 10017

Routledge is an imprint of the Taylor & Francis Group, an informa business

British Library Cataloguing in Publication Data
A catalogue record for this book is available from the British Library

Library of Congress Cataloging-in-Publication Data
Brodie, Kathy.
Sustained shared thinking in the early years : linking theory to practice / Kathy Brodie.
pages cm
Includes bibliographical references and index.
1. Early childhood education. 2. Thought and thinking–Study and teaching (Early childhood) 3. Cognition in children. I. Title.
LB1139.23.B745 2014
372.21–dc23
2013046256

ISBN: 978-0-415-71342-9 (hbk)
ISBN: 978-0-415-71343-6 (pbk)
ISBN: 978-1-315-77449-7 (ebk)

Typeset in Palatino
by Deer Park Productions

Contents

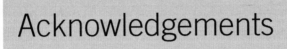

Acknowledgements

Many people have supported and helped me to complete this book, with their insights, wisdom and funny stories of children at play. My sincere thanks to them all.

I would particularly like to thank Annamarie Kino at David Fulton, who has kept me to deadlines and has been wonderfully supportive throughout. As usual, Des Forrest has been generous with her time and has welcomed me into the nursery whenever I wanted to do research or simply to be inspired by the children.

Special thanks go to my incredible family, husband Ian and children Chris and Robs, who have been there for me every step of the way.

Finally, I would like to thank all the children who are a constant source of amazement and delight and who have been kind enough to accept me into their play.

1 An introduction to Sustained Shared Thinking

Thinking is closely involved with the whole child.

(Dowling 2013: 2)

Introduction

Sustained Shared Thinking (SST) has become a buzzword in nurseries and other settings. It is understood by most practitioners to be a good thing, and something that Ofsted is likely to be looking for. Many practitioners can give an outline description of what they feel SST is. However, not all practitioners understand how it underpins almost everything we do with children. It can support work with children of all ages, it supports parents and carers, and it improves the home learning environment.

The different aspects of SST are analysed individually in this book. The underpinning theory is discussed and suggestions for further reading detailed. There are examples and ideas for practice throughout, so practitioners can use SST immediately.

We start off in this chapter exploring some of the concepts behind SST; where it should come from and when it was first coined as a phrase. Practitioners will know that SST is linked to talking with children and actively listening. It is often the most enjoyable part of working with young children, and is something that good practitioners do naturally, without having to be told to or taught how to do it. Children, on the whole, are natural conversationalists who are more than willing to share their ideas, thoughts and views with an attentive and interested adult.

Of course, interacting with children and active listening are not new ideas. Over the years many theorists have advocated this as good practice – from Pestalozzi to Vygotsky and Susan Isaacs to Marion Dowling. There are pedagogical landscapes dedicated to this method, from Reggio Emilia to High-Scope and the mosaic approach. Sustained Shared Thinking differs slightly from these because it has a specific definition, which has come out of longitudinal research, and does not require practitioners to have special training in a new concept. The idea is not new nor is it something 'extra' practitioners have to do with children in their setting.

Sustained Shared Thinking is part of the English curriculum guidance for early years and was first mentioned in the 2008 Early Years Foundation Stage (EYFS), under creativity and critical thinking (practice card 4.3). It also appears in the updated *Development Matters* guidance for the EYFS, stating that 'Sustained shared thinking helps children to explore ideas and make links. Follow children's lead in conversation, and think about things together. Encourage children to describe problems they encounter, and to suggest ways to solve the problem. Show and talk about strategies – how to do things – including problem-solving, thinking and learning' (Early Education 2012: 7).

Reflection

While doing training on SST some practitioners will say one of the challenges is evidencing the dialogues during the busyness of the day. However, SST can be more than just conversations. Last Christmas, the pre-school children chose to do a show based on the *Fran's Flower* book, instead of performing the traditional show. This was because they had been reading the book and had spent a lot of time re-enacting the story in the book corner already. They had been dressing up and talking about all the different foodstuffs, exploring the story in their own way. They had quickly chosen who was to play each part and were asking each day to practice their story and songs. Even after the performance, the children were still dressing up and discussing how Fran had cared for her flower.

Sustained Shared Thinking is demonstrated in this example through the problem-solving of who would play what part, the extended narrative of their own storytelling and the continuous return to the role-play even after the show had been performed.

As a phrase, SST was used in the Effective Provision of Pre-School Education (EPPE) Project which, at the time, was the largest European longitudinal study of pre-school care and education. The EPPE research aims were to try to identify effective pre-schools and compare these with other provisions (and with children who did not attend any type of pre-school provision). Identifying the benefits of the provision, and then measuring how quickly these faded over time, determined the 'effectiveness' of the provision. This was a wide-ranging and detailed piece of research, which had many outcomes, including the analysis of SST and its effect on early education and care. As an interesting footnote, it was decided to use the word 'Thinking' rather than 'Dialogue' or 'Language' (both of which would be possibilities) when describing the interactions between practitioners and children. This came from the grounded theory used during the EPPE research. The coding categories were 'collapsed' (Sylva *et al.* 2010: 155) into Sustained Shared *Thinking* because it came from many, different observable areas that included language, dialogue, adult models and questioning techniques. This demonstrates the breadth of SST and how useful it is in many different circumstances.

Formally, SST is defined as:

> an episode in which two or more individuals 'work together' in
> an intellectual way to solve a problem, clarify a concept,
> evaluate activities, extend a narrative etc. Both parties must
> contribute to the thinking and it must develop and extend.
> (Sylva *et al.* 2004: 36)

By deconstructing this definition, the full implications of implementing and embedding SST can be appreciated.

An episode in which two or more individuals 'work together'.

Sustained Shared Thinking is something that happens between two or more people. This will most frequently be between an adult and a child, but it may also be between children, if one child is a 'more knowledgeable other' (Vygotsky 1978). Sustained Shared Thinking may happen in small groups and is not confined to one to one conversations. The use of the phrase 'work together' underlines the emphasis on it being an active and creative process.

Both parties must contribute to the thinking

This is not the traditional 'teacher' role, where information is presented by the teacher to be simply absorbed, unquestioned by the child. This is a true two-way exchange with information flowing both ways, so the practitioner also learns from the child. It follows the analogy attributed to Plutarch, who suggested that the mind was more 'like a fire to be kindled and lit than a vessel to be filled'. This is the 'shared' element of SST.

An intellectual way to solve a problem, clarify a concept, evaluate activities, extend a narrative, etc.

The thinking element of SST is provided by the content of the conversation and the thought process that goes into it. This may be a practical problem or a theoretical one, such as 'how many bricks do I need to build this tower?' or 'how much does the moon weigh?' Good practitioners constantly explain and expand concepts, making the meaning clear to their children. This could be as simple as 'milk sometimes comes from cows' to more complex concepts such as the solar system or floating and sinking. Most practitioners will constantly evaluate activities in their settings, almost without thinking about it. Those that went well are repeated; those that were not so successful are adjusted.

However, it is less common to find practitioners discussing the activities directly with the children. The one exception to this is the HighScope approach, which has a review of activities at the end of each session (HighScope 2013). It is revealing to discuss activities with children, to find out what they felt the activity was about or how they engaged with it. Sometimes this is at odds with the intended outcomes, but may have provided equally valid learning opportunities. Similarly, extending a narrative helps practitioners to catch a glimpse of the thought processes that young children are using when they are active in the setting.

As the 'etc.' in this part of the definition suggests, this is not an exhaustive list and SST can be applied to everything we do in any setting, at any time. Some more specific ideas and examples are explained in more detail, linked to each area of learning and development in the Early Years Foundation Stage (EYFS), in later chapters.

...and it must develop and extend

This is the sustained part of SST. A problem might be solved, or a concept is explained, but the deep level learning that stays with children and can be built upon, occurs when the thinking is extended. This embeds the knowledge and helps to make it transferable to other circumstances and situations. It may be that the episode is sustained – an activity continued on after snack time for example, but equally 'Sustained' here can also mean that the thought process is sustained. For example, a child may return to a conversation from the previous day, having given it some thought meanwhile. This is the crucial part of SST, which elevates it from a passing conversation to a deep level learning experience for child and practitioners.

Example

Thomas is trying to solve the problem of carrying a long plank of wood out of the small door of the shed. The practitioner encourages Thomas to look at the length of the plank and size of the door. Thomas says 'the door is too little'. The practitioner replies 'Yes, the door is too small for the long plank. What can we do?'

Thomas says 'We could cut it small', to which the practitioner replies, 'What else could we do?' Thomas shakes his head, not sure how to solve this problem. The practitioner gently says, 'Look, it's shorter this way. Maybe we could turn the plank round, so it comes out lengthways?'

Thomas gives this suggestion a moment's thought, and then turns the plank round. Delightedly, he says, 'Look! It goes through now!' With a big smile on his face, he exits the shed with the plank.

When tidying up later on, Thomas realises that the brick box is too wide to fit on the shelf the way he was holding it. After a moment's thought, he puts the box down and picks it up lengthways, presenting the short end to the shelf and sliding the box on easily.

Even in this really small example, the practitioner has learned that Thomas understands size difference and how related problems can be solved. Thomas has been introduced to an alternative solution to a problem and has been able to transfer this knowledge to another situation.

What are thinking skills?

This section investigates exactly what thinking skills mean, in terms of SST. It has already been said that SST is more than just the transference of information from one individual to another; it also involves thinking and communication skills from both parties. White (2002: 99) suggests that 'thinking' is many different activities, which may be described as being directed, undirected, practical and theoretical. Each of these has clear definitions and examples that demonstrate how they may differ. For example, undirected thinking may be called daydreaming or thinking haphazard thoughts, whereas theoretical thinking may be about mathematics or science. Robson (2006: 2), however, uses very different language to describe the thinking process – intelligence, knowing and learning. Taking Robson's first descriptor, intelligence, and investigating this further, it is soon apparent that there are theories of multiple intelligences (Gardner 1983) and even what is meant by 'intelligence' is debated (Roberts *et al.* 2001). Dowling (2013: 2) favours a more holistic approach, linking mind and thought, with 'thinking' being the result of 'processing all the experiences that are received in the mind'. These very different approaches highlight how complex the concept of 'thinking' actually is and how thinking skills can be developed in many different ways.

The thinking skill of a child is one of the areas of learning and development where the competence of the skill does not necessarily directly correspond to the child's age. If a child has been encouraged to think of different solutions and discuss their problems, they will be more skilled at this over time.

Developing children's thinking skills

At the heart of SST is the idea of developing children's critical thinking processes with support from more knowledgeable others. It is a continuous process and is applicable to all activities that a child gets involved in, whether it is in the setting, at home or out and about. It is a powerful way for practitioners to model to children how to 'think about thinking' or metacognition. These sorts of conversations will be happening all the time in settings and homes all over the country. Sustained Shared Thinking supports many areas of child development, including personal, moral, social, emotional and cognitive development and creativity, as described in later in the book.

It is widely recognised that we have little idea of the sort of world our children will encounter as they grow up. Technology, globalisation and world economies, among other things, are changing at such a rapid rate that we cannot hope to accurately teach our children the exact skills they will need for the future. For example, I have spent many hours with children teaching skills with a mouse for the computer, only to find that more and more gadgets have touchpads or touchscreens! However, we can teach children *how* to learn and to have the thinking skills to cope with these changes. Tickell (2011: 87) states that one of the principle determinants of success in later life is 'an ability to be aware of one's own thinking (cognitive strategies, or "skill")'. Therefore, thinking skills should be supported during a child's early years. Sustained Shared Thinking can support this because it encourages the thinking processes. Adults can model the thinking process, where children are unsure about solving a problem or understanding a concept. Equally, adults can learn about how children think about the world and extend this knowledge.

THEORY

Metacognition has been described as 'the ability to reflect upon, comment about, and report a variety of mental states. Metacognition — cognition about cognition — thus forms an umbrella term under which to group such mental phenomena' (Fleming *et al.* 2012: 1280). It is the state of 'thinking about thinking'. It is important for children to develop metacognition so they are conscious of their own thought processes and how they can then apply this elsewhere. By demonstrating their own metacognition, practitioners can support children to understand their thinking processes. Dowling (2013) suggests that practitioners should be explicit about their own thought processes, questioning aloud, explaining sequences and explaining what tasks they are doing. For older children, Dowling advises that the environment is significant, ensuring that children 'recognise the language of thinking and provoking children to think in different ways' (2013: 176) as well as discussing with children the different ways of thinking.

Further reading

Jones, D. (2007) Speaking, listening, planning and assessing: the teacher's role in developing metacognitive awareness *Early Child Development and Care* Vol. 177, Iss. 6 pp. 569 – 579.

This article clearly explains the role of metacognition when working with children and its benefits.

◼ Speech and language

By its nature as a form of communication, SST has very close links with speech and language for the two to five age range, so some theories about speech and language are discussed here, as well as some practical activities to support practitioners.

Speech acquisition in young children is a subject that is discussed frequently and at length. One of the leading theories of how young children acquire and develop speech includes Chomsky's Language Acquisition Device (LAD) (Sheehy 2004), where it is theorised that children are 'hardwired' to acquire language whatever the social situation. This may feel like the case where children simply pick up language under regular circumstances. However, the logical supposition of this theory is that children will learn to talk, even when they have been deprived of exposure to a language. This has been disputed after cases such as Genie (Curtiss 1977 and Rymer 1993) where a young girl, who was deprived of social interaction and language, failed to acquire language skills until she was moved into a supportive environment.

In contrast, Bruner suggested that the LAD 'could not possibly succeed' (Bruner 1986: 77) without a Language Acquisition Support System (LASS) where language is a product of social interactions. Bruner maintains that children need to hear language around them and use language to move from what they can already do, to a more sophisticated use of language.

The communication cycle is incredibly complex. The cycle goes from the point in time when a child is spoken to, through receptive language (which includes listening, remembering, understanding), to expressive language (have an idea of what to say, choose words, choose structure and sound), to speech (physical movement of mouth, tongue) and finally social communication (appropriate speech, eye contact, body language). Every step of the communication cycle has to be right, both in terms of what a child is thinking and of the physical ability to be able to form speech sounds, to be successful.

As adults, we are adept at combining all these steps almost seamlessly. However, young children are still practising many of these elements. When talking to children, especially if challenging children's thinking, practitioners should allow time for children to respond. It is advised that around ten seconds should give a child enough time to listen, choose a response, physically move the mouth and verbalise the response. Try having a friend ask you a question, but wait ten seconds before answering. Does it feel like a long, long time? How long do you normally give children to answer, before asking another question or giving them the answer?

Attending

Attending (as in 'paying attention') is essential for an in-depth, meaningful conversation. Part of this is making eye contact, which focuses the mind on the face. This gives the listener a number of benefits for communication.

- Non-verbal communication from the face, so the child can read the visual cues being transmitted by the speaker. Facial movements are considered to be of 'immense importance in communication' (Coates 2009: 59).
- Lip formations for lip reading (Fox 2011). This is particularly useful for those children who have hearing loss, permanent or intermittent. Eighty per cent of children will have had glue ear at least once by the time they are aged ten (Bupa 2011), and so may only have intermittent hearing. This will not be obvious to the speaker, who may assume the child can hear.
- Reduced distractions. If the child is concentrating on the face, he or she is less likely to be distracted by other people or activity in the room.

PRACTICE

Pre-linguistic activities

Gaining a child's attention and encouraging them to read facial clues is an essential part of communication. You can do this very naturally by playing games with children.

Ready, Steady . . . Go

Set up a 'click-clack' track, where a small car races to the bottom of a track.

Holding the car at the top of the track, say 'Ready, Steady...' but pause before saying 'Go'. Most children will look to your face to find a visual clue or reason for the pause.

When you have the child's full attention, say, 'Go', releasing the car down the track.

This can be done with any toy that will 'go' once released, or even with activities such as bubble blowing, where you blow out the bubbles on 'Go'.

Close to the face

Choose a toy that can be manipulated like, for example, a puppet that pops up or a rainmaker that makes a sound. Hold it close to your face when addressing the child and, once eye contact or attention is achieved, pop up the puppet or turn over the rainmaker. Only use the toy once attention has been drawn to the face.

Communication

Even as babies only a few hours old, children will respond to faces and facial expressions. They will have 'synchronised exchanges of patterns of gaze and vocalisation' (Hargie 2011: 48), meaning that they will match their responses to the speaker's cues. Babies will search for this two-way interaction that is communication. If a baby is denied the reciprocal facial expressions or talk then he or she will become upset and distressed quite quickly.

THEORY

Watch the YouTube clip of Tronick's Still Face Paradigm: http://www.youtube.com/watch?v=bG89Qxw30BM

In this clip, Dr Tronick records mums playing with their babies or young children. The mum chats to her child, face to face, using encouraging vocabulary. The mum is then asked to keep her face 'still', stopping all interactions, but remains sat in front of her child. The child tries all sorts of tricks to get mum's attention, but soon gets distraught, trying ever more demanding tactics. Mum is then told to re-engage and the child soon settles back to play. Interestingly, the video shows the same reaction from young babies to older toddlers, demonstrating that the need for two-way communication is strong even in older children.

Deep level learning

Children's thinking is not only demonstrated through speech and language. By carefully observing the child's actions, a practitioner may learn about the child's view of the world, existing knowledge and previous experience.

THEORY

Deep level learning is when experiences and knowledge 'become more meaningful' (Laevers 2005a: 3). Or, in other words, children can fully understand the implications of an activity and can transfer the knowledge to another situation. This is the type of learning that will be of most benefit for children, because it is transferable and supports learning in other areas of their lives.

Laevers also contends that 'if we want deep level learning, we cannot do without involvement' (Laevers 2005a: 5). He has formulated a five-point scale (Laevers 1994) that describes the different levels of involvement. The scale points range from one, which is low level passive activity with little cognitive demand, to five, which is sustained intense activity with energy, concentration and persistence. Children that rarely have the higher levels of involvement are unlikely to be experiencing deep level learning either.

These are the experiences that move children's learning on and extend their knowledge. The development may be as small as a new word learnt or a whole theme or topic being developed from an episode of SST. The critical aspect is that it is a process, which should be improved and built on over time.

THEORY

Quality and quantity of language

Research from iCan, the children's communication charity, has shown that it is important that children hear plenty of language to stimulate their communication. However, the type of language 'has been shown to be equally important' (Freeman and Hartshorne 2009: 5). This includes having a range of language types as well as positive reinforcement.

In terms of SST, the research also showed that one very important element is the 'quality of the interaction rather than the quantity' (Freeman and Hartshorne 2009: 8). This highlights that SST should have a shared purpose and 'working together'.

Moral development

Moral development, or developing the ideas of actions that are right and wrong, is usually just emerging in pre-school children. Children in their early years start to 'actively construct their moral judgements' (Kanira and Ward 2013: 261) and it was an area that Piaget (1965) linked to cognitive development. Nucci (2008 :1) states that 'Piaget viewed moral development as the result of interpersonal interactions through which individuals work out resolutions which all deem fair' and that the adult's role is to give children the opportunity to discuss their feelings. Sustained Shared Thinking gives children the opportunities to clarify the concepts of fairness and discuss the problems associated with what is right and what is wrong. It also gives practitioners the opportunity to explore seemingly contradictory situations. For example, it is OK to run outside, but not indoors. Occasionally there are some children who have different rules, for reasons such as Special Educational Needs or personal circumstances, and this can be communicated effectively to the other children using SST.

Personal development

Personal development can be considered to be the sense of self and the sense of others. By sharing thoughts, ideas and extending activities, children begin to realise that others have different views to their own. This is termed theory of mind (ToM) and is defined by Goldman (2012: 402) as 'the cognitive capacity to attribute mental states to self and others'. Being able to understand your own mental state and that of others gives children the basis for good personal development, such as self-esteem, self-confidence, empathy and resilience.

Resilience is defined as 'emotional self management' (Goleman 2006: 166) or the ability to cope with the difficulties that are encountered in life. There is growing research (Panter-Brick and Leckman 2013) to show that good resilience will have positive, life-long effects. Perry and Szalavitz claim that 'resilient children are made, not born' (2006: 38) and they go on to explain how different life experiences can help or hinder this process. The role of SST in supporting personal development, therefore, is to model for children the processes and strategies to help build some of these personal attributes. The detailed discussions about how children themselves feel and how others might feel supports the children's thinking processes, so they can transfer these skills to other circumstances. Sylva *et al.* in their book explaining the EPPE research, *Early Childhood Matters*, explain how their research found that 'Sustained Shared Thinking also encourages children to be curious and adept at problem solving' (2010: 231).

Layout of the book

Each chapter examines a different layer of SST. They are designed to support practitioners and students in every aspect of their work, whether that is working in a setting or writing an assignment. The underpinning theory has been separated into boxes, for easy reference for students and those more interested in the theoretical side. Suggested further reading has been included within these boxes so students can analyse the concepts in more detail. Sometimes the readings support the point and sometimes they are an alternative viewpoint, to allow critical analysis.

Examples are used throughout to illustrate the points for practitioners and are drawn from experience. There are also practical ideas separated into distinct boxed Practice sections, so practitioners can quickly find ideas for activities in the setting and students can use these ideas on placements. The Reflection boxes are personal examples of SST in different contexts, illustrating how SST may look in your practice or setting.

Each chapter has been closely linked to the EYFS (DfE 2013) so practitioners in England can make the connections between the theories and practice easily. It should be noted that the good practice will also be applicable to other curricula in the UK, for example, the value of play and SST, how a close and caring adult can support SST and the importance of the home learning environment.

▓ Some points that are expanded on later in the book

One concern that is often raised is whether practitioners are doing SST 'correctly'. This is explored in detail in Chapter 5: 'The role of the practitioner and key person', where both pedagogy and practical examples are discussed.

Play is very important for children's development. In Chapter 6, the value of play and how it supports, and can be supported by, SST is investigated.

Sustained Shared Thinking with children who have Special Educational Needs (SEN) is analysed in detail in Chapter 7. Some of this commentary may also be relevant to children who just need a bit of additional support in their lives at this particular time.

A note on the language used. 'Teaching' is used as a term throughout the book. I do not intend to suggest this is the formal 'teaching' that could be imagined in a school classroom with older children – sat in rows at desks completing worksheets. I am using this term in a much more general way to mean educating, instructing, supporting, scaffolding, mentoring, coaching and the myriad of different techniques that a skilled practitioner may use.

▓ Conclusion

Sustained Shared Thinking is about process, not product. Talking to the child is about sharing information, enjoying and being absorbed by the moment, not getting to the 'right' answer – in most cases there will not be an answer.

This method of talking with children, learning from them and exploring their interests in depth is a powerful way to gather knowledge about interests, worries and worldview. More importantly, SST encourages metacognition and supports personal, social and emotional development. It is something that practitioners will be doing without thinking. Doing more of it will scaffold children's development even further.

2 How Sustained Shared Thinking can support the Characteristics of Effective Learning

> Curiosity is the engine of achievement.
>
> (Sir Ken Robinson 2013)

Introduction

This chapter starts to examine the role of SST in the Early Years Foundation Stage (EYFS), and where SST can support other areas of children's learning and development. The chapter focuses on some of the concepts within the Characteristics of Effective Learning as defined by the EYFS (DfE 2012). This includes an investigation of theories about 'creativity' in young children and play theories, highlighting where SST may be used to support these. The chapter also explores the concept of 'tuning into the child' and, in particular, how this supports development. Many of these concepts are common to other curricula, particularly creativity and active learning.

The Early Years Foundation Stage

The EYFS in England has two components. Firstly the statutory component, which contains everything early years providers must do to meet their legal obligations (DfE 2012). This includes the welfare and safeguarding frameworks for settings. The second component of the EYFS is the guidance, which consists of suggested good practice and advice, including an indication of age appropriate development. This guidance is called *Development Matters* (Early Education 2012) and describes the Characteristics of Effective Learning (CofEL) and the seven areas of learning and development. The CofEL underpin the rest of the guidance material. Generally, when practitioners refer to 'the EYFS' they are referring to both components, without differentiating between the two. This is because they are nearly always used as complementary documents, each with a specific function.

The *Development Matters* component (Early Education 2012) can be considered to be the 'what' that is desirable to be achieved with children aged 0–5 years old. This culminates in the EYFS Profile, usually completed towards the end of the Reception year. The Profile is a snapshot of the child's developmental stage at that particular time. The information is used for statistical analysis across England and as a measure of the progress made by children in Reception classes.

In the *Development Matters* document each area of learning and development is subdivided into three columns – 'unique child' is guidance as to what the child is learning, with the other two columns – 'positive relationships' and 'enabling environments' – giving ideas of how this can be achieved. Up until the revised *Development Matters* was issued, the missing piece in the guidance documents was the rationale, the 'why', it is good practice. Without this, there was the temptation to create a 'ticklist' from the EYFS, checking children's development as a series of box-filling exercises, without understanding where these have come from or seeing the holistic nature of the child's development. Practitioners have always been aware that children rarely, if ever, develop in neat stages across all levels, so it is still debated as to whether it is appropriate to compartmentalise children's learning into neat areas in this way. In addition, there is little agreement as to what the stages should be or how these can be attached to age ranges. In order to highlight the holistic nature of the *Development Matters* document, it is stated on every page that:

> Children develop at their own rates, and in their own ways. The development statements and their order should not be taken as necessary steps for individual children. They should not be used as checklists. The age/stage bands overlap because these are not fixed age boundaries but suggest a typical range of development.
> (Early Education 2012)

The Characteristics of Effective Learning give an explanation for why the guidance is good practice and the holistic development, rather than individual areas of learning and development, that it is supporting.

The fact that different 'areas of learning and development' are prescribed from country to country, even within the UK, calls the Piagetian stages of learning and development into question. Does a child start to develop differently, under different areas of learning, because he or she has moved from

England to Wales? Even the expectations and achievement levels differ from country to country. For this reason it is vital that the development of children is considered holistically, wherever they may be in the UK.

In addition to the Characteristics of Effective Learning and the seven areas of learning and development, there are some attributes that practitioners should support the development of in their children. For example, adaptability and self-regulation are critical attributes for today's children, who will be adults in a very different world to the one in which they are growing up or the world in which practitioners grew up. The explosion in technology and its ease of use is one small example of how the world has changed, and how children must adapt to keep up. Stewart (2011) notes the importance of encouraging self-regulated learners in such an uncertain society.

Characteristics of Effective Learning

The *Development Matters* document starts with the four themes (a unique child; positive relationships; enabling environments; and learning and development) that are familiar to the original EYFS in 2008. The four themes work together:

- a unique child being used to observe how a child is learning;
- positive relationships are what adults can do to support and encourage this;
- enabling environments are the environments that adults can provide;
- these add up to learning and development for the child, which is recorded under Piagetian-type ages and stages.

The Characteristics of Effective Learning (CofEL) are a new addition to the revised *Development Matters* document and they 'support children's learning across all areas' (Early Education 2012), underpinning both Prime and Specific Areas. Dame Clare Tickell first gave them form in her review of the EYFS in 2011 (Tickell 2011: 26), describing them as being 'critical for building children's capacity for future learning'. She explained them as 'a short description of how each child demonstrates the three important characteristics of learning' (2011: 34). The CofEL are:

- playing and exploring;
- active learning;
- creating and thinking critically.

Sustained Shared Thinking is part of the 'positive relationships' column of the creating and thinking critically category, although the principles run throughout the whole of thinking critically.

A good way to remember this is as 'hands' (playing and exploring), 'heart' (active learning) and 'head' (creating and thinking critically). The origins of this model may be Petrie *et al.* (2006: 22), whose research suggested that 'the work of the pedagogue [involves] the whole human person: head, hands and heart'.

Playing and exploring – hands

The EYFS defines playing and exploring as 'children investigate and experience things, and "have a go"' (DfE 2012: 7). It is based around the theories that say that children learn best by having real-life, concrete experiences. This is not a new idea – Froebel, 150 years ago, designed and manufactured his 'gifts' for children so they could experience different concepts according to a sequential system (Weston 2000). Montessori, 100 years ago, 'stresses the education of the senses' through the environment and experiences that are planned for the children (Bruce 2005: 33). More recently, Laevers defined experiential learning as 'exploiting and enhancing the energy in people and drawing them into a positive spiral which engenders deep level learning' (Laevers 2005a: 9).

Sustained Shared Thinking supports experiential learning through extending narrative and learning together between practitioner and child. Children can extend and embed their learning by discussing their experiences with practitioners. This could be in a formal way, such as the HighScope methods, where children plan their activity, do the activity (have the experience) and review it afterwards. Or this may be more informal, where the practitioner encourages SST during the activity, discussing what is going on, drawing inferences and suggesting extensions to the play.

Theorists have been urging the importance of play for many years. As time progresses and more research is carried out, it seems to be becoming more obvious that a child's play is not only desirable, but it is necessary. Whitebread (2012: 5) states in his recent research that 'playfulness is strongly related to cognitive development and emotional wellbeing'.

Active learning – heart

The EYFS defines active learning as 'children concentrate and keep on trying if they encounter difficulties, and enjoy achievements' (DfE 2012: 7). It is closely linked to dispositions, where children are aiming for a mastery disposition,

THEORY

Experiential Education (EXE)

Experiential Education (EXE) evolved in Belgium during the 1970s and 1980s. It is based on the Leuven Levels of Wellbeing and Involvement, developed by Laevers (2005a). One of its key aims was to develop children into 'creative' adults. Since the inception of EXE, there have been four outcomes that have defined its success.

1. Emotional health. Children have shown good levels of self-esteem, self-confidence and resilience.

2. Nurturing the child's exploratory drive. Children are self-motivated and demonstrate deep-level learning, rather than shallow competencies.

3. Valued competences and dispositions. Competences are viewed as life skills and development is holistic in nature. This fits well with the ideas of mastery dispositions in the EYFS.

4. Preserving 'linkedness'. Laevers describes this as a connectedness that can 'prevent destructive and anti-social behaviour (delinquency)'. It is about how children view themselves as part of a wider community and, ultimately, a global society.

In sum, Experiential Education sees wellbeing and involvement as a measure of deep learning and of the effectiveness of the learning environment.

Adapted from: Laevers (2011: 2)

Further reading

Constable, K. and Green, S. (2013) *Planning for Schematic Learning in the Early Years: A practical guide*. London: Routledge.

This book gives an unusual insight into experiential learning and its links with schematic play.

and active learning theories. Active learning can be defined as 'learning where the learner is responsible for instigating, planning or managing what they do' (Scottish Government 2010:1). This is a powerful way of learning, for anyone at any age, but particularly for young children where habits for life can be formed. Learning in this way has overlaps with experiential learning, where the child can start to form their own meaning from their own experiences.

Practitioners should remember that different children will take away different meanings and learning from the same experience. So one child may enjoy the feel of the glue, one may enjoy the glitter and one may learn how to mix paint colours – all from the same painting and gluing activity. This is also the reason for repeating activities, so children can get further learning from different aspects of the activity.

In her evaluation of the EYFS, Dame Tickell reported that 'self-regulation is a concept that involves attitudes and dispositions for learning (the motivation, or "will"), and an ability to be aware of one's own thinking (cognitive strategies, or "skill")' (2011: 87). This combination of 'will' and 'skill' can be supported very successfully through SST. The motivation (will) is supported through praise, encouragement and active listening. The ability to do something (skill) is supported through problem solving and joint learning between the practitioner and the child. Active learning also supports some of the factors that foster resilience in young children, namely: a positive disposition, positive self-concept, balance between independence and interdependence (David *et al.* 2003).

Reflection

Mastery disposition and problem solving go hand-in-hand. Having the perseverance to keep trying, even when you have failed the first time, is a skill that will always stand you in good stead for the future. Even very young children can demonstrate to you how to try, try and try again.

Jacob, who was just 14 months old, was playing with the wooden fort. He had wanted to get the soldier out of the fort, through the front gate, and over the drawbridge. In order to do this he had put his hand through the front gate, from the outside, and grasped hold of the soldier. However, now he had a problem. The soldier and his fist were too big to draw back out through the front gate. At this point, Jacob could have put his hand over the top of the wall and simply have lifted the soldier out the fort. But he was quite determined that he wanted the soldier to come across the drawbridge, as soldiers should do. I watched him as he tried again and again, grasping the soldier and trying to get his fist through the gate that was far too small. He must have done this over half a dozen times before he thought for a moment and then put his other hand into the fort, pushing the soldier's head out through the gap. He could now grasp the soldier, making him march across the drawbridge.

Jacob was totally absorbed in his activities and totally unaware of me watching him, fascinated, to see how he would solve this problem. However, his ability to sustain his thinking and solve the problem was exceptional.

Active learning is also closely linked to SST through the 'conscious act of thinking' (Scottish Government 2010:3), meaning that children have to really consider and absorb their experiences. Sustained Shared Thinking supports this through discussion, extending theories and concepts. It encourages children to make connections between their experiences and embeds learning. Practitioners can gather information about the types of things that children have learned. Together, practitioner and children can then move the learning forward. This may be through other activities, such as taking the learning outdoors, or related concepts, such as repeating the activity using different materials.

THEORY

Dispositions

Children's dispositions are much discussed and debated in early years' research. They are closely linked to the ideas of active learning and that children have the 'heart' or 'will' to learn. Claxton (2007: 5) defines a disposition as 'merely an ability that you are actually disposed to make use of', whereas Katz and Chard (2000: 26) use 'habits of mind' for describing dispositions and the way that children learn. The example they use is reading – a child may have the skills to be able read, but may not have the disposition to pick up a book. Clark (2001:229) explains how dispositions are inseparable from feelings and can be 'nurtured, extinguished, or damaged according to how they are affected in the learning situation. Ignoring feelings that accompany the learning process may damage the disposition to learn'. Sustained Shared Thinking can support these feelings, by acknowledging the child's achievement in a genuine and interested way.

Dowling (2010: 24) describes how dispositions can affect learning and the links between mastery dispositions and self-esteem. Dispositions can be supported or dismissed, according to the way in which children are treated. Einarsdottir *et al.* (2009: 224), while investigating children's drawings, found that 'where dispositions such as creativity and persistence are rewarded, children are likely to regard drawing as a pleasurable activity'. With even the briefest of SST, children's creations can be encouraged, building both mastery disposition and self-esteem. Practitioners may also learn what it is that motivates the child and encourage this in the future.

Claxton and Carr (2004: 90) describe how 'children's persisting, questioning or collaborating can develop in flexibility and sophistication' depending on how much support the children get in their environment. This reflects the ideas of SST, particularly the questioning and collaboration, and demonstrates how the skills of the practitioner can help to support the child's learning.

Claxton (2007: 3) further developed these ideas, producing a list of dispositions that effective learners should have:

- curious, adventurous and questioning;
- resilient, determined and focused;
- open-minded, flexible, imaginative and creative;
- critical, sceptical and analytical;
- both methodical and opportunistic;
- reflective, thoughtful and self-evaluative;
- keen to build on their products and performances;
- collaborative but also independent.

THEORY

An interesting and revealing test of disposition and later resilience is the Marshmallow test. This is a classic test where a child is given a marshmallow. The child is asked to wait alone in the room with the marshmallow for a few minutes, without eating it. The child is told that if they DON'T eat the marshmallow, they will get another one later, and they can eat both. The researcher leaves the room.

After leaving the room, the researcher watches the child to see what they do. Do they distract themselves, sniff the marshmallow, lick it or simply eat it (forfeiting the second marshmallow)?

Goleman (1998) relates how, in the original test, some children waited, using a range of self-distraction techniques and had the reward of two marshmallows, while others ate their marshmallow. When the progress of both sets of children was followed up, 14 years later, the researchers found that those children who had waited (delayed gratification) had more resilience and were more socially secure than those who couldn't wait.

This deceptively simple experiment demonstrates how children's dispositions will have an effect later on in life and how these may be predicted from a very early age.

For some YouTube clips of children doing this test (and some very amusing results!) see: http://www.youtube.com/watch?v=QX_oy9614HQ

Creating and thinking critically – head (or mind)

The EYFS defines creating and thinking critically as 'children have and develop their own ideas, make links between ideas, and develop strategies for doing things' (DfE 2012: 7). This is the place in the EYFS where SST is mentioned by name and highlighted as being good practice. However, it could be argued that SST is implicit in all areas of the CofEL.

Children's thinking, how it links to learning, self-esteem, self-confidence, personal, social and emotional development, as well as other areas of development, is a constant source of research and fascination. Dowling (2013: 3) suggests that it is important to consider young children's thinking for three primary reasons:

1. strong support from research evidence;
2. imperative in the National Framework;
3. increased insights from practitioners in their day-to-day work.

As we have already seen, SST comes from research and has subsequently been shown to support children. Although SST is mentioned by name only in the EYFS guidance, rather than the EYFS statutory document, it is considered good practice. The main strength of SST, using these three reasons, is that it increases insights for practitioners about the children in their care. By exploring, in depth, an idea or concept, practitioners can really understand how the children see the world, how they construct their understanding and how this can then be supported further in the setting and the home learning environment.

Both Sir Ken Robinson (2009), and Mihaly Csikszentmihalyi (2002) before him, have interviewed adults about finding their passion for work and how this has affected their lives. They both found that people's creativity and depth of thinking was greatly increased when they were doing something that they enjoyed. This created a sense of happiness and harmony, creating a virtuous cycle. Interestingly, even though the two authors interviewed very different people, at different times and in different parts of the globe, they both surmised that anyone could find their passion, and transform their lives. This is interesting because this is exactly the type of creativity and critical thinking that practitioners are being encouraged to foster in young children (i.e. not the 'creativity' that is cutting and gluing a picture). This creativity is about developing and really investigating ideas and concepts. It is linked to criticality because it is an analysis or evaluation of concepts and experiences. As an idea, this is not unique to the UK. Fumoto *et al.* (2012: 4) suggest that this is international, where 'at policy and curricular level, there is clear evidence of the valuing of creativity, and of supporting young children's creative thinking, of both its present and future importance in their development'.

More recently, Robson and Rowe (2012: 349) investigated young children's creative thinking, with a particular focus on engagement, involvement and persistence. They found that creative thinking was just as evident in activities such as gardening and construction as it was in painting. However, they found that outdoor play and 'socio-dramatic play were particularly effective contexts'. The role of the practitioner was significant, with adults influencing children's creative thinking more than children influencing each other. Practitioners were also better at encouraging children to speculate. Most interestingly, though, they found that 'interactions between children more often supported higher-level thinking than interactions between adults and children' (2012: 363). The implication of this piece of research for SST is that interactions between children should be encouraged and supported. Sustained Shared Thinking should not just be reduced to an interaction between one adult and one child; it is much more than that. It could also be that children challenge and stretch each other more than adults do.

THEORY

Leuven scale of involvement

Ferre Laevers, from the Leuven University, has developed a pair of scales that describe children's wellbeing and involvement. These give practitioners descriptions as a guide to how children are feeling. Both are produced here, but the scale of involvement is 'closely allied to the Characteristics of Effective Learning' (Veale 2013: 90). This is because children's creativity tends to increase with their level of involvement, as well as persistence and thinking critically.

TABLE 2.1 Leuven scale for wellbeing

Level	Wellbeing	Signals
1	Extremely low	The child clearly shows signs of discomfort such as crying or screaming. They may look dejected, sad, frightened or angry. The child does not respond to the environment, avoids contact and is withdrawn. The child may behave aggressively, hurting him/herself or others.
2	Low	The posture, facial expression and actions indicate that the child does not feel at ease. However, the signals are less explicit than under Level 1 or the sense of discomfort is not expressed the whole time.
3	Moderate	The child has a neutral posture. Facial expression and posture show little or no emotion. There are no signs indicating sadness or pleasure, I comfort or discomfort.
4	High	The child shows obvious signs of satisfaction (as listed under Level 5). However, these signals are not constantly present with the same intensity.
5	Extremely high	The child looks happy and cheerful, smiles, cries out with pleasure. They may be lively and full of energy. Actions can be spontaneous and expressive. The child may talk to him/herself, play with sounds, hum, sing. The child appears relaxed and does not show any signs of stress or tension. He /she is open and accessible to the environment. The child expresses self-confidence and self-assurance.

TABLE 2.2 Leuven scale for involvement

Level	Involvement	Signals
1	Extremely low	Activity is simple, repetitive and passive. The child seems absent and displays no energy. They may stare into space or look around to see what others are doing.
2	Low	Frequently interrupted activity. The child will be engaged in the activity for some of the time they are observed, but there will be moments of non-activity when they will stare into space, or be distracted by what is going on around.
3	Moderate	Mainly continuous activity. The child is busy with the activity but at a fairly routine level and there are few signs of real involvement. They make some progress with what they are doing but don't show much energy and concentration and can be easily distracted.
4	High	Continuous activity with intense moments. The child's activity has intense moments and at all times they seem involved. They are not easily distracted.
5	Extremely high	The child shows continuous and intense activity revealing the greatest involvement. They are concentrated, creative, energetic and persistent throughout nearly all the observed period.

Further reading

For further reading about the Leuven Scales and Ferre Laevers, this is a very accessible and user friendly guide:

Laevers, F. (Ed.) (2005b) *Wellbeing and Involvement in Care: A Process-oriented Self-evaluation Instrument for Care Settings.* Research Centre for Experiential Education: Leuven University.

Conclusion

Throughout the Early Years Foundation Stage it states that, in both the statutory framework and the guidance, children develop holistically, at their own rate and as individuals. However, the EYFS is a way of describing children's learning in general, so practitioners are aware of 'typical' development patterns. The EYFS is the statutory framework by which settings are legally bound. Children's learning and development are detailed in *Development Matters*, which is underpinned by the four themes.

The three Characteristics of Effective Learning are:

- playing and exploring;
- active learning;
- creating and thinking critically.

These can be described as children learning using their 'Hands, Heart and Head'. Sustained Shared Thinking is specifically mentioned in 'Creating and Thinking Critically' (Head). This type of creativity is much more than painting a picture or gluing. It is creativity of ideas, concepts and experiences and involves critical thought, with depth of perception. Sustained Shared Thinking as a strategy is particularly good at supporting this because it aims to extend ideas and thoughts. Because it occurs between two or more people, learning can be moved on. However, SST can equally be used while playing and exploring or during active learning. These are common themes through many of the curricula of the UK, so SST is a useful tool for many practitioners who are supporting children's learning.

3 Sustained Shared Thinking in the Prime Areas

Three areas are particularly crucial for igniting children's curiosity and enthusiasm for learning, and for building their capacity to learn, form relationships and thrive.

(DfE 2012: 4)

Introduction

In this chapter the focus is on the Prime Areas of learning and development, as defined by the revised EYFS (DfE 2012). These are: personal, social and emotional development (PSED), communication and language (CL) and physical development (PD).

Each Prime Area is considered separately to highlight where and how SST may be incorporated into the curriculum, drawing extensively on the *Development Matters* document (Early Education 2012). For each area there is some background theory, practical ideas for practitioners and further reading on the subject. Although in this chapter and the following chapter, the areas of learning and development are discussed individually, it cannot be stressed enough that all the areas are interwoven and are interdependent on each other. A child's development should be considered holistically, not just as a box that must be ticked. All areas of learning and development will impact on the others, to a greater or lesser extent.

Context

It is very easy to become submerged in the curriculum that you use every day, without thinking too much about how it could be different elsewhere. Even within the UK there are four different curricula and, although there are similarities, there are some significant differences too (see the following Theory box). The differences indicate some of the character of the region that they serve. The Welsh Foundation Phase includes Welsh Language Development. This is part of the Welsh Government's commitment for a 'truly bilingual Wales' where children 'have the right to feel a sense of belonging to Wales and to enjoy experiences in and of the Welsh language' (Department for Children, Education, Lifelong Learning and Skills 2008:5). Both Northern Ireland and Scotland specify religious education as an area of learning and development. England is the only region to have a totally separate strand for literacy development.

Although practitioners may see differences in their day-to-day working if they started using a different curriculum, the overall aim of supporting children across a range of development would be very similar.

THEORY

Variations in the curricula of the UK

Each area of the UK has different areas of learning and development, according to its early years' curriculum. The Welsh Foundation Stage and the Scottish Framework both have separate frameworks for the under threes, England's framework is for the nought to fives and Northern Ireland for the nought to sixes. So already the curricula show differences in ideas about child development stages and how children's stages vary.

TABLE 3.1 Variations in the curricula of the UK

Welsh Foundation Phase	Northern Ireland Curriculum	Scottish Curriculum for Excellence (CfE)	English Curriculum (EYFS)
Personal and social development	Personal development and mutual understanding	Health and wellbeing (social studies)	Personal, social and emotional development
Physical development	Physical development and movement	Health and wellbeing (social studies)	Physical development
Wellbeing and cultural diversity	Religious education	Religious and moral education	
Language, literacy and communication skills	Language and literacy	Languages	Language and communication
Mathematical development	Mathematics and numeracy	Mathematics	Mathematical development

(continued)

TABLE 3.1 Variations in the curricula of the UK *(continued)*

Welsh Foundation Phase	Northern Ireland Curriculum	Scottish Curriculum for Excellence (CfE)	English Curriculum (EYFS)
Knowledge and understanding of the world	The world around us	Sciences	Understanding the world
Creative development	The arts	Expressive arts	Expressive arts and design
Welsh language development		Technologies	Literacy

The variation in the classification of areas of learning and development demonstrates the importance of considering development holistically.

Variations in the curricula around the world

Internationally the curriculum is even more varied, with some curricula choosing not to have specific learning 'outcomes' but more holistically desirable attributes for the children. For example, in Finland they do 'as little measuring and testing as they can get away with' (Levine 2011: 1), although there is a core curriculum that schools have to follow. Teachers have much more freedom and are trusted to deliver a suitable curriculum, which tends to be more holistic than other curricula.

Not all countries see the need to have different curricula for early years and older children. For example, the Swedish curriculum goes from pre-school up to age 16 (Year 9) (Skolverket 2011). There are signs that some of the UK curricula are also following this lead, with the latest Scottish curriculum going from pre-birth to 18 years old. The idea of a continuum of development over the whole of 'childhood', served by one, seamless curriculum, fits well with the concepts of the holistic child. It also relieves the pressure to attain targets or goals by a predetermined 'stage' or when children transition from one curriculum to the next. This allows practitioners to concentrate on the more important, underpinning development, such as personal, social and emotional development.

THEORY

Sweden: an example of one international curriculum

In Sweden, the 'pre-school' (förskola) is available for children aged one to five, after which they attend kindergarten (förskoleklass) until they reach compulsory school age at seven years old. The pre-school curriculum is based on a value system, which 'focuses more on basic values such as playing together, tolerance and consideration for others' (Swedish Institute 2012). There are some parallels to be drawn with other curricula. For example, there is an emphasis on the links between pre-school and home, cooperation between pre-school and school as well as children's development and learning.

All these are preceded by the underpinning norms and values, defined as 'Education should impart and establish respect for human rights and the fundamental democratic values on which Swedish society is based' (Skolverket 2011: 9). Goals are not age related and are universal for all children. For example, by the time children leave compulsory schooling they can:

- consciously determine and express ethical standpoints based on knowledge of human rights and basic democratic values, as well as personal experiences;
- respect the intrinsic value of other people;
- reject the subjection of people to oppression and degrading treatment and also assist in helping other people;
- empathise with and understand the situation other people are in and also develop the will to act with their best interests at heart;
- show respect and care for both the immediate environment, as well as the environment from a broader perspective.

(Skolverket 2011: 14)

Further reading

For further insights into the Swedish curriculum, read Chapter 11 in Nutkins, S., McDonald, C. and Stephen, M. (2013) *Early Childhood Education and Care: An Introduction*. London: Sage.

The English Curriculum

In England the EYFS (DfE 2012) has a Piagetian curriculum, which is based around the ages and stages that children typically develop. The curriculum is designed for children from birth to five years old. There are seven areas of learning and development, which have been divided into three Prime Areas and four Specific Areas. Although all the areas are considered to be interconnected, the Prime Areas are identified as being 'particularly crucial for igniting children's curiosity and enthusiasm for learning, and for building their capacity to learn, form relationships and thrive' (DfE 2012: 4). The three Prime Areas are: communication and language, physical education and personal, social and emotional development. The Specific Areas are: Literacy, Mathematics, Understanding the World and Expressive Arts and Design. The Specific Areas are explored in the next chapter. As we have already seen, these are arbitrary, and sometimes misleading, divisions of children's learning and development, which depend on the social and cultural context in which they exist. In addition, there are many other theories of development and 'intelligence' that fit none of the child development categories (see the following theory box).

THEORY

Multiple intelligences

Practitioners should be aware of the idea of multiple intelligences. Howard Gardner has researched and written extensively about multiple intelligences (1983, 1996) and how these will vary over time according to experience. He suggests there are eight distinguishable intelligences:

1. linguistic;
2. musical;
3. logical-mathematical;
4. spatial;
5. bodily-kinaesthetic (dexterity, motor control and hand-eye coordination);
6. intrapersonal personal intelligence (introspective, one's own feelings);
7. interpersonal personal intelligence (looking outwards to others feelings);
8. naturalistic intelligence (nature and outdoors).

These are very different from the standard 'intelligence' that is measured in, for example, an IQ (Intelligence quotient) test. However, when working with children, these should all be considered, as well as the areas of learning and development in the *Development Matters* guidance. There are some obvious overlaps (linguistic and communication and language; bodily-kinaesthetic and physical development) but Gardner's multiple intelligences also identify some areas not in the EYFS. For example, nature and outdoors and musicality are small subsets of other areas of learning and development.

Communication and language

The methods by which children learn to talk and communicate are much debated. Many theorists have some beliefs about language acquisition in young children, how this happens and why it happens. Sometimes the theories are at odds with each other, but there are some core concepts for supporting language development that are well established.

THEORY

Genie

Noam Chomsky (1965) originally theorised that humans are born with a Language Acquisition Devise (LAD) that means that humans have a predisposition to talk and use language, whatever their cultural or social upbringing. He did adjust his ideas to include Universal Grammar some years later. There were some criticisms of Chomsky's ideas because the best way to prove them would be to deprive a child of hearing language at all during the beginning of their life, and then see if they develop language after the first few years of life – termed the 'critical period' for language development – had passed. Obviously this is an ethically and morally impossible 'experiment'. However, in 1970, in Los Angeles, the scientific world was presented with just such a child.

'Genie', as the girl was named, had been kept for her first 13 years locked away and alone, rarely spoken to and not exposed to social situations of any sort. She was the ideal case study to help understand how language could develop after the critical period had passed. Genie acquired vocabulary quickly, more quickly than had been anticipated, but her communication developed along atypical lines. For example, her grammatical constructions and syntax did not develop as would be expected. Genie helped scientists understand language acquisition; particularly brain lateralisation (how the two hemispheres of the brain interact) but still left many unanswered questions.

Several other theorists have discussed why some children are so much more proficient at language acquisition than others. Bruner (1983) adapted Chomsky's theory with his own theory, which he called Language Acquisition Support System (LASS). This suggests that children learn language from adults (or others who are more knowledgeable in language), who scaffold the child's learning. He postulated that language was a social development, supported by parental (or adult) input, and needed to be collaborative, so both parties could share meaning. This would certainly seem to be what was missing in the case of Genie, who had none of this scaffolding, and had no language.

Further reading

Find out more about 'Genie: Wild Child' on YouTube: http://www.youtube.com/watch?v=JOVY-52YmjE (last accessed 5 October 2013) or read Rymer, R. (1994) *Genie: A Scientific Tragedy.* New York: First HarperPerennial.

For more information on Bruner's theories, read Bruner, J. (1983) *Child's Talk: Learning to use Language.* New York: Norton.

How SST can support communication and language development

The practitioner's role when supporting communication and language is to support, scaffold and model good language. How this is done depends on the age and level of development of the child, as well as their personality and preferences. For example, you would use a very simple sentence structure and simple words for a young child, but for a school-aged child, you may use metaphors or complex sentence structures.

PRACTICE

For very young children and babies, games such as peek-a-boo are excellent for catching the child's attention and modelling turn taking. This can be achieved by using a silk scarf or piece of material over the practitioner's face. As this is removed, the practitioner says something (such as 'peek-a-boo' or the child's name), to get the attention of the child. Although very simple, these games form the basis of a two-way conversation because the baby is focusing on the face and anticipating speech – prerequisites for communication. Repeating this many times can increase a child's concentration.

For toddlers, it is important to model good conversation and show that you are really listening to their contribution, using positive body language and active listening. Items of provocation are a good way to start a conversation. You can do this a number of ways:

● hide an item and allow the children to discover it;

● 'discover' the item yourself to start the conversation;

● gradually set up the discovery over a number of days by, for example, creating a trail of glitter one day, tiny footprints the next, a tiny wand the next, etc.

● ask parents and carers to bring in interesting objects.

The objects should be open-ended enough to provoke questions and allow the child or children to start making some guesses as to the source of the item. Some good items to use are:

● glitter;

● peacock feather and other feathers (ensure they are clean);

● acorns and their cups;

● a giant footprint in the mud (or cut out of black paper);

● interesting shells and stones with a hole through the middle.

Items of provocation may work with some older children, but some may feel that they 'know the answer' which doesn't promote conversation as well. For these children, you may be better asking the children to explain how something works or the game they are playing (if this does not interrupt their play). Older children generally love to explain the rules of the game they have made up, or how they have set up a play area. Practitioners should be especially sensitive to listen and not be tempted to 'correct' the play.

Physical development

Of all the areas of learning and development, physical development is one that practitioners are most likely to consider to 'just happen'. It seems that children grow from babies to toddlers to pre-schoolers, getting bigger and growing stronger with minimal assistance. Practitioners need to simply provide opportunities and watch for any 'significant gaps' (Greenland 2013: 169) in development, where they can provide support.

However, some of the most physical activities need preparation and thought before they can be achieved. For example, what equipment is needed to build an obstacle course, how many children can safely play football at the same time? Bilton (2004: 25) gives a case study where the group of children had to work out how to raise a bucket of stones using a simple pulley system. By posing challenging situations and then supporting children to solve the problem together, using SST, the children have had to 'think, try out and adapt in the light of their findings'.

THEORY

Aspects of physical development

Greenland (2013: 170) states that physical development and movement supports 12 distinct, although interwoven, areas of development:

1. to develop the feel of things and a subjective sense of self;
2. to organise sensory information and develop perceptual abilities;
3. to connect the parts of the body and the feel of the whole of the body;
4. to build relationships;
5. to create tactile experiences;
6. to gain a sense of where limbs are;
7. to develop a sense of balance and equilibrium;
8. to develop motor skills;
9. mobility;
10. to acquire physical mastery;
11. moving to be seen;
12. to embody life and learning.

It is hardly surprising that physical development is a Prime Area when it supports so many different areas of development.

Further reading

For more details about normative physical development, the book *Integrated Working with Children and Young People: Supporting Development from Birth to Nineteen* (London: Sage), edited by Nadia Edmond and Mark Price (2012), has an excellent chapter covering this.

How SST can support physical development

Practitioners should be aware of their own physical movements and attitudes towards physical development. Modelling a positive attitude and using positive language towards physical activity encourages children to become involved. Doherty and Bailey (2002: 70) believe that this can also 'foster their skill development'. Practitioners can use SST to support and encourage children. By discussing their individual challenges, such as trying a new game outdoors (gross motor skills) or persevering at a jigsaw puzzle (fine motor skills), practitioners can help children move onto the next level of development. This can be extended into negotiation about imagination and role play (Cooper and Doherty 2010), which are not obvious areas of physical development, but contain elements of this. For example, setting up a stage or getting all the picnic items outdoors can be quite a physical challenge.

Greenland (2009: 48) states that 'Children are biologically driven to move in certain ways'. As practitioners, if we ignore this, we risk reducing a child's capacity for self-confidence, self-esteem and their natural desire to communicate. This could be running down the corridor, climbing the fence or balancing on the wall. Practitioners should both acknowledge and support babies and young children who are on the move. This can be through extended conversations about risk, hazards or appropriate movement indoors. Although, unusually, this type of SST has an ultimate aim (to keep the children safe in their environment), it is a valuable way of exploring the children's attitude to risk and physical movement. It can also be extended into children suggesting safer ways of achieving the same aim.

PRACTICE

Practical activities

'This Little Piggy' and other rhymes where the practitioner touches the child and names the body part helps the baby or child to associate the body with the word. This can stimulate conversations about the body and names.

Young children naturally gravitate towards playing on the floor. Try moving the table and chairs to one side and having all the activities on rugs (to define play areas) on the floor. With older children you can discuss the room layout and how the toys are going to be distributed.

You could also use the underside of the table. Attach paper underneath the table, so children can lie on their backs to draw or mark make. You can join the children under the table, discussing their mark making with them.

Personal, social and emotional development

Personal, social and emotional development (PSED) is the bedrock of learning and needs to be supported by sensitive and caring adults. The DCSF document – *Social and Emotional Aspects of Development (SEAD)* – (2008b: 5) states that PSED forms the 'building blocks of future success in life' and 'has a huge impact on later wellbeing, learning, achievement and economic circumstances'. It goes on to define personal development as 'being me', social development as 'being social' and emotional development as 'having feelings'. Babies having a secure attachment to a loving adult supports PSED and gives them a firm foundation from which they can build other relationships and start to learn.

THEORY

Attachment theory

John Bowlby (1969) researched and developed the concepts of attachment theory. He was initially interested in how children react and adapt to separation from their families, or important family figures, whether due to hospitalisation, homelessness or enforced separation. At the time he was researching, the prevailing psychoanalytical theories were about the child's views of their mothers (Klein 1932), rather than the relationships that actually existed. Bowlby strongly believed that it was the relationship with the mother (or other, permanent caregiver) that was critical to the mental wellbeing of children. He also suggested ways of mitigating the ill effects of separation.

By 1950, Mary Ainsworth was assisting Bowlby with his research. She developed the 'strange situation' experiment (Ainsworth and Bell, 1970). A child is observed playing happily with their mother in a room. A stranger enters the room and the mother leaves. The mother then returns after a short period of time. Ainsworth and her team observed the child's behaviour both when the mother leaves the room and when she returns. They found that the child's reactions differed and the differences could be explained using the tenets of attachment theory. Extending the research, they also found that the behaviours varied according to the situation, describing them as being 'heightened in situations perceived as threatening' (Ainsworth and Bell 1970: 64).

From the research, Bowlby concluded that having a secure attachment to a caregiver (mother or other carer) was vital to a child's future emotional development. However, not all children made secure attachments. Bowlby described three types of attachment.

1. Secure. This is the attachment behaviour that most children will display. It is emotionally healthy and is displayed as the child in distress after a brief separation, but the child is comforted and settled by the caregiver.

2. Anxious/avoidant. After a separation, the child will not readily return to the main caregiver and, in more severe cases, even prefer to go to the stranger.

3. Anxious/resistant. This is a display of more complex behaviour, with the child sometimes going to the caregiver, but also resisting contact. Sometimes this is associated with violent behaviour, but overly passive behaviour may also be seen.

Main and Soloman's research (1986) identified a fourth attachment category – insecure/disorganised (also known as disoriented) attachment. As the name suggests, the child has indiscriminate responses to separation from the caregiver, displaying a range of resistant, avoidant and apprehensive behaviours.

Further reading

Perry and Szalavitz (2006) describe the consequences of not having a secure attachment in their book *The Boy who was Raised as a Dog*. The book is a series of case studies, where poor attachment and lack of emotional bonding affects the developing brain, sometimes with devastating consequences. These examples demonstrate how important it is for children to have an attachment figure in their early years of life.

Aubrey, C. and Ward, K. (2013) 'Early years practitioners' views on early personal, social and emotional development'. *Emotional and Behavioural Difficulties* Vol. 18, Iss. 4 pp. 435–447.

How SST can support personal, social and emotional development

The areas of personal, social and emotional development are closely related and reliant on each other. They are based on the child's self-esteem and self-confidence. Although the two are linked, they are separate aspects of a child's (or adult's) personality. Self-esteem is the internal feelings we have about ourselves, while self-confidence is our external personality that we show the world.

Sustained Shared Thinking can be vital in supporting self-esteem in young children. Dowling (2010: 17) suggests that a child's self-esteem is 'totally dependent on the people who matter to her and the situations that they provide'. This may be as simple as children having an adult actively listen to them for the first time, or to take one of their suggestions seriously. For some children self-esteem is built through the knowledge that their shared involvement in an activity has solved a problem or created something new.

Reflection

Sometimes working with children who have personal, social and emotional additional needs can mean that you have to think differently. I was finding it very difficult to have conversations with a young girl, pre-school age, who had a chaotic home life and needed significant support with her PSED. She almost point-blank refused to be drawn into a conversation or to engage in activities for any length of time. This was beginning to seriously worry me, as I felt I was unable to give her the support she desperately needed before really knowing her own personality.

I had tried to tempt her into conversation in different areas of the setting and at different times of the day. One day, I was lying on my back within the triangular mirror box, with some of the toddlers, laughing at our many reflections and how they moved when we waved. Suddenly, I noticed that my pre-school girl had joined me, lying down at the other end of the triangle so we were head to head. She also started waving and seemed to be absorbed by all the many images of herself and how they were distorted in the reflections of a reflection. Gradually, I started commenting on how I could see her in so many different places and how we looked different upside down. She started to talk to me, just about the reflections and who she could see in the triangle with us. It was the first time she had engaged in any type of extended conversation with me.

After that, whenever we wanted to have a conversation, we would get the cushions and go and lie on our backs in the triangle looking at each other's reflections. In this way she could talk to me, and see my reactions, without having to have face-to-face conversations, which were obviously still problematic for her.

Self-confidence is built through support given by adults. Dowling (2010: 23) classifies four responses that encourage and develop children's self-knowledge or self-confidence. These are:

1. clarifying – this is paraphrasing and repeating back a child's idea or thought to help the child to move the thinking along;

2. asking for information – showing genuine interest in the things that the child has to say;

3. providing information – understanding the child's achievements and giving genuine encouragement;

4. use of silence – to allow the child time to formulate a response and for the adult to be respectful enough to wait until the child is ready.

The first three responses are closely aligned with SST, even using some of the same terminology. The use of silence would, at first glance, appear to be different. However, if the practitioner is practising true SST then allowing the child to formulate their thoughts is a natural part of this.

PRACTICE

Practical ideas

Communication is more than talking, as babies who sign can prove. By using simple signs (either ones that you have made up and that you can both understand, or using standard signs) practitioners can start to communicate and support very young children. Baby sign benefits are said to include:

● reduced frustration;

● building confidence and self-esteem;

● stimulating intellectual and emotional development.

(Adapted from Sing and Sign, 2013)

For older children, using drawings and art is a good way to start conversations. For example, drawing around a child on a giant piece of paper and adding objects and people who are important to the child, either as photos or drawings. While doing this, the practitioner can talk about the chosen items without it feeling like an interrogation.

Similarly, you could engage in SST with children to find out what they would bury on a treasure island, particularly good for children who like pirates!

Puppets are an excellent way for a shy or cautious child to talk. Many children who find it overwhelming to talk to adults will happily chat to a puppet lion or dog, especially if the practitioner joins in the fun and uses a suitable voice to reply in. The practitioner can use puppets to have SST with a range of children, and puppets can work well with small groups and SST.

Empathy dolls are used to support every child's everyday feelings (as opposed to persona dolls that tend to support more difficult situations such as biting or transitions). They help children to identify and explore their own feelings and to build empathy for others as well. These can be used as a starting point for SST about empathy or can be used to support a child with discussing their problems.

Further reading

For more information about empathy dolls, read *Using Empathy Dolls* (2009, London: A&C Black) by Kirstine Beeley, who explains their use as well as why it is so important to foster empathy in even our youngest children.

Conclusions

There are many ways of supporting the Prime Areas in the EYFS through SST. Communication and language is the most obvious area that can be supported, but the examples given demonstrate how the other Prime Areas can also be supported.

The examples are to give practitioners ideas for starting SST, although it can be used in many different ways.

4 Sustained Shared Thinking in the Specific Areas

Specific Areas include essential skills and knowledge for children to participate successfully in society.

(Early Education 2012: 4)

Introduction

This chapter explores the other four areas of learning and development in the EYFS guidance, *Development Matters*: Literacy, Mathematics, Understanding the World (UW) and Expressive Arts and Design (EAD). These are the more socially and culturally constructed areas of learning and development but still have equivalence with the other curricula of the UK; Mathematics, in particular, appears in all curricula.

The Specific Areas have some more challenging aspects of SST. Expressive Arts and Design and Understanding the World are usually linked closely to children talking about their experiences and sharing their insights. For example, children represent their ideas through stories (EAD) and they talk about features of their environment and about changes (UW) (Early Education 2012).

However, practitioners rarely associate Mathematics with SST, with the exception of precise mathematical phrases. Similarly, the focus of Literacy tends to be the written word, phonics and spellings. In both cases, practitioners can start to grasp children's *understanding* of the concepts by engaging in SST. For example, it is reasonably simple to determine whether a child can add one more to a given number. However, working out why a child is unable to do this is much more complex – is it because the number names are muddled up, or the word 'more' is misunderstood ('more juice' and 'one more' are very different things!), or that the child actually doesn't want one 'more' pencil? By discussing this in a sustained way, and not just ticking the box for 'no understanding', the reasons may be unravelled. Once this has been achieved, the practitioner can start to work on correcting misunderstandings or presenting the task in a way in which the child will engage.

▧ Mathematics

Traditionally, the Piagetian view of mathematical learning is that children have to be a certain age before they can understand mathematical concepts such as, for example, conservation of mass (Piaget and Inhelder 1969). However, further research indicates that mathematical learning has many different dimensions, which can be supported in different ways. Gifford (2004) suggests a multi-sensory approach is essential, along with social learning and modelling. She also promotes the use of 'Discussion: negotiating meanings, "shared thinking" and open-ended questions' (Gifford 2004: 111).

THEORY

Mathematics in the Early Years

There is research that shows how important discussion is for mathematical development. Mercer and Sams (2006: 525) showed how important 'the quality of dialogue between teachers and learners' is. They also demonstrated that use of language improves conceptual understanding.

In 2007 Sir Peter Williams was asked to review mathematics teaching in Early Years settings and primary schools. He found that children must 'talk about their developing mathematical understanding' and that effective pedagogy required 'practitioners to support, challenge and extend children's thinking and learning through sustained shared thinking and use of accurate mathematical language' (2008: 34).

Williams made several recommendations, including that practitioners should model open questions and mathematical language in their dialogue with children and that this would come from 'discussions of solutions, exploration of reasoning and mathematical logic' (2008: 38). Mix *et al.* (2011) have expanded on this, commenting on how supporting language could improve understanding of one-to-one correspondence.

Further reading

Professor Robert Siegler has been writing and researching for almost four decades on children's mathematical and scientific thinking. You can find dozens of selected articles and lots more information at: http://www.psy.cmu.edu/~siegler (last accessed on 8 October 2013).

How SST can support Mathematics

Maths is more than just counting and numbers. The Early Learning Goal in *Development Matters* (Early Education 2012: 36) for shape, space and measure includes size, weight, capacity, position, distance, time, money, patterns, shapes (3D and 2D) and problem solving. This is a massive spectrum of ideas to incorporate into one area of learning and development, particularly when it includes such abstract ideas as time and money. Critically, children are expected to be able to discuss these concepts, using both 'everyday' language and 'mathematical' language. Sustained Shared Thinking is therefore essential to support this area of learning and development. The deep level, extended conversations are needed to both model mathematical language and to determine whether children have an understanding. Particularly as the language we use when discussing concepts has a specific meaning and is not always what we would use in our everyday conversations (Robson 2012).

Reflection

While doing some observations in a large, private day nursery I noticed that many of the children's files had little or no entries under the 'mathematics' area of learning development. When I asked about this, the deputy manager told me that this was because practitioners were not confident with maths themselves, so did not feel confident doing it with the children.

During my day at the nursery, I witnessed practitioners doing complex calculations on how many members of staff were needed at lunchtime to cover for lunches, because there are different ratios for children under two and for the over twos. Similarly, the practitioner who was working out how much pasta to cook for their lunch had to allow for the children who were not having pasta, those with smaller appetites and the older children. Another practitioner had to calculate how long it took to set up an activity and whether there was enough time for every child to take part if they wanted to. The practitioner laying out the sleeping mats had to work out how much floor space was needed to accommodate all the children comfortably.

When I pointed out to the deputy manager the ways in which her members of staff were using maths all the time, without knowing it, she was pleasantly surprised. Speaking to the practitioners afterwards,

I encouraged them to make their maths visible to the children by discussing the sorts of things they were doing all the time. This not only encouraged the children to understand that maths is an everyday tool, rather than something scary, but it also showed the practitioners how adept they were at maths themselves.

PRACTICE

Just a minute...

So-called 'everyday' mathematical language can be very confusing, and in some cases contradictory. Think about the sort of language that you use all the time when talking to children:

- How often do you say to your children 'I'll just be a minute' or 'please wait a minute'? How often is this *actually* a minute?
- When is a cup 'full'? Do you mean full, right to the top, or just full enough to drink out of? Similarly, when is a cup 'half full'? Did you check it was exactly half the total capacity of the cup?
- When is money 'a lot'? Does a police car cost 'a lot'? Compared with a chocolate bar, it probably does, but compared with a helicopter, it may not.
- How can a large, shiny copper coin be 'less' than a small, dull silver coin?
- Who lives the 'closest' – Grandma or Nanna? It only takes 10 minutes to get to Grandma's house in the car, but it is a 20-minute walk to Nanna's house.
- Where is the teddy? He has been left behind. Is this the same 'behind' as 'watching Dr Who behind the sofa' or 'we are running behind time with snack'?

It is essential to consider the language that you use with the children and the meaning that it conveys. As children's understanding develops, they will be able to distinguish the meaning according to the context in which a word or phrase is used. However, until you are sure of this, always check that your children understand your meaning.

Sustained Shared Thinking can demonstrate how much children can understand about maths, and how much of the knowledge they can transfer to other situations. When engaging in SST and maths, make sure to make these links explicit, and explain how 'one more' can be 'one more dog', 'one more pencil', etc.

Expressive Arts and Design

Expressive Arts and Design is what used to be Creative Development in the 2008 Early Years Foundation Stage (EYFS). Creative Development was very often translated as creativity with paints, 3-D modelling, drawing, etc. However, there are many ways that children can be creative. This could be through music, drama, language, role-playing and storytelling. The new Expressive Arts and Design title reflects this breadth in children's development. Bruce (2004: 2) states that 'We can cultivate creativity in every baby, toddler and child' and she goes on to explain how the different layers of creativity can be nurtured in our children.

Sometimes, the difficulty is not a lack of creative thoughts and ideas, but being able to make the children's thinking visible. Carefully recorded observations, plenty of photographs and practitioners who are tuned in to creativity can help ensure that creativity in any form is not overlooked.

THEORY

Recently Dr Teresa Belton has claimed that boredom can foster creativity by making children use their internal stimulus, rather than relying on constantly being entertained by a screen (Richardson 2013). The research was based on interviews with creative individuals who recalled how being bored in early childhood meant that they became self-reflective, made up stories to amuse themselves or had to try activities, such as baking, for the first time. It is very tempting as practitioners to always keep children active, with a constant stream of new things to try. However, this research shows that creativity doesn't need this, and it could even be that we are blocking creative time by filling it with other activities. Isbell and Raine (2012) identify four dimensions of creativity:

1. the creative person;
2. the creative process;
3. the environment that nurtures creativity;
4. the product of the creative act.

The complex nature of creativity can be investigated by using these four dimensions in observations and assessments.

Further reading

Read more about Dr Belton's research in *Primary Leadership Today* magazine.

Sir Ken Robinson has made a series of inspirational lectures about creativity in all its forms for TED (Technology, Entertainment and Design). These can be found on the TED website: http://www.ted.com/speakers/sir_ken_robinson.html

He has curated a selection of 10 other TED speakers on education, who are also incredibly interesting.

How SST can support Expressive Arts and Design

Sustained Shared Thinking supports Expressive Arts and Design by helping practitioners to understand children's thinking and their creativity in thought. By recording these dialogues, either in writing, audio or video, their creativity can be captured.

PRACTICE

There are plenty of ways to share creative materials with babies, whether it is the feel of paint, different textures of materials or bubbles in water. The interactions, such as making eye contact, talking and showing enjoyment, will form the basis for later talking. Things such as baby copying your movements or solving a problem together such as scrunching up paper and then flattening it out again can demonstrate the shared thinking.

Many babies enjoy listening to music. Sustained Shared Thinking can be used to support this by actively listening to music together (not just having it on in the background), moving together to the rhythms and singing along together.

Toddlers can really enjoy making up songs and music. You can use SST to find out the type of music they would like to play (happy, sad, fast, slow, loud, soft, etc.) and then to discuss how this will be achieved. Will they need the CD player, or make their own instruments? How many children will be playing? During the performance, SST can be used to resolve any issues between children, if there are musical differences!

For many older children plays and storytelling are an important part of exploring their imagination and creativity. It is a way to reconstruct or play out previous experiences, to explore what it may feel like to be someone else or to construct social situations to their own agenda. Sustained Shared Thinking can be a vital part of the exploration of a theme for a play or the structure of a story. By discussing at length and in detail what happens next or the sequence of events, practitioners may begin to understand the child's point of view and to support learning.

▨ Literacy

Literacy in *Development Matters* (Early Education 2012) is subdivided into reading and writing. For young babies, this seems to be irrelevant, but there are many things that practitioners can do to lay the foundations for reading and writing such as, for example, giving children a love of books and demonstrating the difference between pictures and words.

Young children need to understand that there can be communication between two people, whether it is spoken, sign language or other forms of communication. Then, they must understand that there are symbols (writing) that can be used to represent this communication. Stone and Stone (2007: 5) suggest that there is a literacy continuum, which must be completed before a child can read. This is a movement from symbolic play to representational thought to reading. They theorise that play provides 'the means for the child to progress through the stages of representational development necessary for literacy'.

This highlights two important aspects of literacy:

1. It is based in communication. You will often hear practitioners talk about 'writing for a purpose', meaning that the children are making a shopping list or writing a letter to grandma. The purpose is to communicate an idea or thought, such as what to buy or a 'thank you'. Writing will be meaningless until children can understand that language (of all varieties) is a communication.

2. Writing or written symbols are a representation of something – an idea, a piece of information, an instruction. Children must have an idea about what that 'something' is before they can start to use the symbols to represent it.

Sustained Shared Thinking supports both of these aspects because it strengthens the child's ability to communicate a thought or idea and encourages children to take this further, creating new ideas, concepts and solutions.

THEORY

Literacy projects

There are many early literacy projects, but one of the most enduring is probably the Raising Achievement in Early Literacy (REAL) project, led and championed by Professor Cathy Nutbrown (Nutbrown and Hannon 2011). The project started in 1995, in Sheffield, and aimed to work with parents to promote the literacy development of pre-school children, while supporting the parents with their own literacy. The feasibility of the methods used was assessed and the most effective methods were then disseminated to practitioners and policy makers.

The philosophy of the project is that literacy is a family issue, with both children's literacy and parents' and carers' literacy 'inextricably linked' (Nutbrown and Hannon 2011: 3). The ORIM framework – Opportunities, Recognition, Interaction and Model – was used to plan and explore different areas of early literacy.

Since 1995, the project has been developed and used effectively in many areas. For example, in 2009 the Early Childhood Unit at the National Children's Bureau (NCB), in conjunction with the University of Sheffield, Sheffield and Oldham Local Authorities, developed a three-year project, 'Making it REAL', based on the ORIM framework.

The PEEP (Parents Early Education Partnership), an early intervention charity based in Oxford, uses the ORIM framework for its parent partnership programmes (PEEP 2013). Their aim is to improve educational attainment through a structured programme of activities and information sharing with parents. This is rooted in good practice for early literacy from the REAL project.

The importance of the REAL research was recognised in May 2013, when Professor Nutbrown was awarded the ESRC (Economic and Research Council) Award for research that had an 'Outstanding Impact in Society' for her work with the ORIM framework and Early Literacy (University of Sheffield 2013).

Further reading

For further information about REAL and ORIM, there is a website: http://www.real-online.group.shef.ac.uk

How SST can support literacy

Literacy is defined by UNESCO as the 'ability to identify, understand, interpret, create, communicate, compute and use printed and written materials associated with varying contexts' (UNESCO 2013). It is more than 'decoding' or making sense of the squiggles on the page. In the twenty-first century it is as likely to be about making sense of digital texts as it is about paper books.

Literacy includes the richness of storytelling and communication, as well as creating written media and interpreting the written word. Flewitt (2013: 4) highlights how phonics teaching alone will not create 'fluent, motivated and critical readers'. She suggests that 'early literacy is viewed as beginning at birth and unfolding in babies' everyday experiences, with family members as role models for language and communication within community networks of rich literacy practices'. This can be extended further to include practitioners as role models for literacy, as well as parents and carers. Sustained Shared Thinking helps practitioners to give children rich literacy practices.

PRACTICE

Sharing books with even the youngest children can prompt questions about the story, pictures, things that make the children laugh, the fact that a story has a beginning, middle and end, etc. These can lead naturally to discussion and SST. Books can be shared with a group or with individual children.

Oral storytelling can be magical for children. You can draw children into the story by using the child's name and weaving the story around the child's own interests and experiences. This can be an excellent way to set up SST, by getting to a point and asking your child what they think would happen next, or asking them to explain a part of the story. This is a good technique to engage children who are shy or who are reluctant to stay in one place for SST.

Poems and reciting from memory can be effective ways of cueing children into listening to different words. Rhyming words, homonyms, phonemes, etc. can all be investigated. Sustained Shared Thinking around the sounds that words make can be a very valuable basis for early literacy and reading.

Many young children now make use of iPads and other electronic reading devices, with books loaded onto them. These can't show children how to turn the pages of a book, or have the wonderful array of size, shape, lift-the-flaps features that other books have, but they can foster a love of stories. Interactive digital books are a good way to start a conversation, especially if the child is more able to use the technology than the adult!

Going on an environment print walk is a good way to start conversations about what children can see. By simply pointing out letters that are the same as the letters in the child's name you can start a conversation about names, words, font, size, etc.

▥ Understanding the World

Understanding the World, of all the areas of learning and development, has the most diverse remit – from people and communities, to 'the world' and technology. It is closely linked with Bronfenbrenner (1979) and the many links that children (and parents) have with their home, community and the wider world.

THEORY

Cultural differences

Park and King (2003) discuss how politeness between adults and children in East Asia and North America is viewed differently. In Korea, children must use the correct honorifics to denote the appropriate social hierarchy between the speakers. They state that 'if a child does not use the appropriate verb endings to express respect to an adult, the adult will be offended, and the child will be reprimanded for rudeness' (2003: 1). Similarly, Khmer families in Cambodia would expect their children to greet their elders in the proper manner and to address other people in the correct way, according their relative social status.

In many Western cultures adults will use more basic speech patterns and words with children, even altering the pitch of their voice – so called mother-ese. However, this is not universally the case. Kulick (1992) found that the natives of the Papua New Guinean village spoke very little to their youngest children, because they were not considered to be 'conversational partners' (1992: 191) (adapted from Park and King 2003).

While investigating how parenting programmes may need to be adapted to suit the culture of the participants, Lubell *et al.* (2008) found that there were some consistent core values, but also some significant differences. For example, each group 'wanted their children to be respectful, obedient, and polite; to share and to do well in school; and expressed displeasure with their children being disrespectful, disobedient, selfish, dishonest, or having temper tantrums' (2008: 13). However, not all cultural groups agreed on the type of discipline or tactics they would use when their children digressed. Some cultural groups preferred 'time-out' while others felt that it made no difference, or that it made the child feel 'insecure' (2008: 11).

Further reading

Stiera, J., Tryggvasonb, M., Sandströmc, M. and Sandbergd, A. (2012) 'Diversity management in pre-schools using a critical incident approach'. *Intercultural Education* Vol. 23, Iss. 4 pp. 285–296.

This is an interesting study from Sweden, which concerned intercultural competence and how pre-school teachers should be consciously aware of their own cultural behaviour.

How SST can support Understanding the World

Most practitioners would be culturally sensitive to play, the types of toys used and activities that are offered to children. This has to be extended to SST. For example, practitioners should be aware of the cultural norms of the children they are caring for when talking with and to adults (see the Practice box below). By being sensitive to these sorts of issues, practitioners can communicate more readily with children, and they will also promote self-esteem and self-confidence in their children.

PRACTICE

Making photo albums of a child's family and extended family is a good way to keep the family in mind when a child is at the setting. Even from a very young age, children will recognise themselves and their family in a photo. Take some photos and stick them onto card. Laminate or cover with sticky-backed plastic. Punch two holes in one side of each photo and tie together with ribbon or string. It is a good idea to record who is in the photo (especially if it is 'Grandma' or 'Nanna'!), where it was and the date it was taken. This helps you to talk to your child with more relevant details.

Review the 'home corner'. Does it reflect the homes that all children will recognise? For example, the home corner for a travelling family may look very different to a traditional home corner. You can use SST to discuss with the children the sorts of things they have at home and what they would like to see in this area to reflect it.

The outdoors environment offers lots of opportunities to discover the world. Is the weather the same everywhere? What does the landscape look like elsewhere? This can be investigated through children's own experiences of travel or through images and videos on the computer or the practitioner's own arte-facts and photos of travelling. For older children this could lead onto map making, growing exotic flowers or fruit (why do we have to bring this plant indoors in the winter?) and discussions about the birds and beasts elsewhere.

Further reading

Pauline Allen's book has loads of interesting and different early science projects arranged in logical groups. This book is particularly good for pre-school or reception: Allen, P. (2012) (2nd Ed. updated by Debbie Chalmers) *Science and Technology for the Early Years: Purposeful play activities.* Dunstable: Brilliant Books.

Conclusions

The many ways that SST can support the Specific Areas of learning and development have been examined in this chapter. Mathematical development can be problematic, partly due to practitioners' own insecurities, and partly because we tend to use mathematical terms in a non-mathematical way.

Understanding the World is a massive area and encompasses a wide range of interests, some of which the children will have more knowledge of than the practitioners like, for example, places they have visited.

Sustained Shared Thinking in the Specific Areas has wide appeal, with plenty of rich sources of interest to explore.

5 The role of the practitioner and key person

Parents and other caregivers teach young children by paying attention and interacting with them naturally.

(Gopnik 2009: 4)

Introduction

This chapter investigates the attitudes, knowledge and understanding that a practitioner, and in particular the key person, must adopt in order to start or maintain successful SST. The role of a reflective practitioner, and how this will help to support SST, is also explored here.

We have already seen how practitioners can support children in the different areas of the English Curriculum, the EYFS, using SST. It should be noted that this depends on having practitioners who are attuned to the children and their interests. Dowling (2013: Glossary) defines attunement as 'being on the same wavelength as the child'. This is more than knowing about where the child is developmentally such as, for example, if he or she can count reliably to five. Instead it is a deep understanding of the types of interests that fire the child's imagination. This not only informs the practitioner's SST but can also be used for assessment. For example, Glazzard *et al.* (2010: 74) state that 'nothing informs assessment like knowing how to be together, where challenge is not threatening (or driven by targets) but exciting and rewarding (and driven by motivation and a sense of creative thinking)'. This description of working together and creative thinking is very suggestive of SST.

The role that the practitioner and/or key person plays is therefore vital because this person is the most likely to be attuned to the child and the child's interests. Laevers (2005a: 8), when discussing wellbeing and involvement, goes further, saying 'the personality of the teacher is even more important than other dimensions of the context, such as the space, the materials and the activities on offer'. Therefore, this chapter investigates the different techniques and roles that practitioners play to ensure that their knowledge of the child is used to its full extent.

■ The ways in which practitioners can support SST

There can sometimes be confusion from practitioners about what SST actually feels like. Obviously each piece of dialogue between two participants (whether it is child-adult or child-child) is unique, and it may be useful, but it is not always classed as SST.

Example

Note that merely repeating back what has been said to you is not SST.

Ella: 'I got red balloon.'
Adult: 'Yes, you've got a red balloon.'
Ella: 'It's mine!'
Adult: 'Is it yours?'
Ella: 'Yes.'

This conversation does not extend a narrative or solve a problem. There has only been limited learning, in that Ella has confirmed that the balloon belongs to her, which she probably already knew. It is not extended or sustained.

To make the above dialogue into SST it would need to be extended. For example:

Ella: 'I got red balloon.'
Adult: 'Yes, you've got a big red balloon.'
Ella: 'It's mine!'
Adult: 'Is it? Where did you get it from?'
Ella: 'From the party.'
Adult: 'Tell me about the party.'
Ella: 'Kirsty's birthday.'
Adult: 'Is it Kirsty your cousin or Kirsty from nursery?'
Ella: 'From nursery, with Alyshea and Hannah. I had cake and water but Hannah had juice. I don't like juice.'
Adult: 'What do you like to drink best?'
Ella: 'Water and milk ... milk at home, my mum makes, cos it's warm.'

By extending this conversation the adult has learned about friendships that are important to Ella, her drink preference and also that her mum makes her milk warm. The adult could take this further by either investigating the party (more about the friends who had been there, what did they do, etc.) or about the ways that things differ between nursery and home (do you have a cup like the ones at nursery, what do you have for snacks at home?).

Michael Jones (Jones 2013) describes how talk between two people may come in four categories:

1. small talk;
2. chat;
3. banter;
4. conversation.

The intensity and depth of conversation increases through the categories, from small talk to conversation, with SST being firmly in the conversation category. Jones describes this type of discussion as 'where two or more people share ideas in-depth about topics that are really important to all concerned'. Although all four categories still have a place in settings, it is important that practitioners can differentiate between small talk, chat and banter, and the in-depth conversations of discussion and SST.

When SST first appeared in the EYFS, on the practice card 4.3, it was stated that 'Sustained shared thinking can only happen when there are responsive, trusting relationships between adults and children' (DCSF 2008a). This is normally a given in most settings. However, practitioners should be aware that if a child is only just building those relationships such as, for example, if they are new to the room or a new child joining a child-minder, then the child may be reluctant to have in-depth conversations. Once the trust and understanding has been built up, then the SST will happen more naturally. Practitioners should be aware of building relationships before rushing in to create opportunities for SST.

Robson (2006: 133) explains how Vygotsky suggested that there is conceptual development that is 'formal', or learned as part of schooling, and 'everyday', which is learning in context or as part of everyday life. Both types of learning are important; they build upon one another and are complementary. The temptation is for some practitioners to focus on the formal development; asking children set questions, ticking boxes against

Reflection

Just as children are unique so practitioners are too. We all have our own strengths and weaknesses, our own preferences and dislikes. I have had practitioners say to me that 'babies do nothing', but then there are practitioners at the other end of the scale who cannot tear themselves out of the baby room and are only happy when they have a gurgling baby on their knee.

The importance of having practitioners with different interests was brought home to me recently when I visited a nursery at lunchtime. The babies were being fed in their highchairs and were happily eating their lunch. The practitioner was engaging with them, giving them eye contact and encouragement.

However, when another practitioner, who is a big fan of babies and likes nothing better than giving them cuddles, came into the room the babies' faces lit up and they became very animated. Immediately the practitioner responded to this by coming over and chatting to them, making exclamations as to how well they were doing eating their lunch, sitting in their chairs and drinking their water. In turn, the babies started 'chatting' back, waving their spoons and kicking their legs. This piece of SST was taking place because this particular practitioner had a special connection with this age group of children. The mutual animation and sheer enjoyment between baby and practitioner really gave these conversations depth and meaning. These conversations lasted many minutes, probably over ten minutes. Although previously the babies were happy, their eagerness to engage in a shared conversation with this practitioner demonstrated to me the importance of choosing the right practitioner for the right job role.

developmental milestones. The everyday learning can sometimes be valued or encouraged less often. Sustained Shared Thinking can be used to support both types of learning, with the information from the in-depth conversations used to inform assessment and development. However, in formal situations, practitioners must be careful not to terminate the conversation once the 'correct' answer has been given, but to ensure that the conversation reaches a natural conclusion. Similarly, learning that is demonstrated in an everyday situation should be valued and supported as much as a formal learning opportunity.

Example

Nazmin is getting out the paper for her friends to draw on. As she hands out the paper, she says 'one for you, one for you and one for you', giving one piece of paper to each friend. When she has finished, she stands back and says, 'That's one, two, three ... and one for me – four!' Here, Nazmin has demonstrated one-to-one correspondence and adding one more.

Harri is in the car with his mum and the two dogs. He asks his mum, 'How many are there in the car?'
She replies, 'Two'.
Harri says, 'No, there's four – two of us and two dogs'. Harri is demonstrating here how dissimilar objects can be counted, and an addition of two.

Both of these examples are 'everyday' learning, but both demonstrate a clear understanding of mathematical concepts, without sitting the children at a formal learning session. In both examples the depth of the child's knowledge could be further explored by engaging them in SST.

Pedagogy and ethos

Pedagogy is the way that we teach children, or educate them, combined with the way that we support their development, such as personal, social and emotional development. It is based on a holistic view of the child and is a much wider role than the traditional 'teacher' that you would find in a school. Moss and Petrie (2006) theorise that pedagogy is an attempt to address the whole child. The ethos of a setting is the principles or ideals that underpin the education and care of the children. Sometimes there is a strong ideology that influences the environment, teaching, toys, etc. such as the Montessori or Steiner philosophies. But, even if the setting doesn't follow a prescribed philosophy, there will still be an encompassing philosophy of some sort. This is sometimes articulated as a mission statement, but sometimes it is simply the 'feel' of the setting or 'how we do things here'. When reflecting on the EPPE research, Sylva *et al.* (2010: 160) found that any setting, whether it is a nursery, crèche or out of school club, benefitted from a strong lead and a strong philosophy. They go onto to describe how 'the managers of the excellent centres ... valued the importance of adult-child interaction and supported their staff to develop better ways of engaging children'.

It is interesting to review both the pedagogy and the ethos of the setting to see how they may affect SST. For example, is the pedagogy one that favours the more 'academic' areas, such as literacy? Or is the pedagogical approach based around listening to each other? Similarly, does the ethos encourage practitioners to take time and listen to the children? It is worth making an action plan, with the rest of the staff, if you discover that the pedagogy does not encourage and support listening to children. While exploring the quality of training of practitioners in the EPPE research, Sylva *et al.* (2010: 163) state that practitioners 'need to develop a deep understanding of the pedagogical principles if they are to develop expertise in applying them in a wider range of collaborative teaching and learning contexts'. It is not clear whether the teacher training at the time (2003) achieved this or not. Another of the outcomes from the EPPE research was the creation of the Early Years Professional Status (EYPS), which has now been revised into the Early Years Teacher (Teaching Agency 2013). This Status was originally developed to meet the pedagogical challenges that were perceived in early years' settings at that time. It will be intriguing to see if subsequent research shows the type of impact that the EYPS or Early Years Teachers have had on pedagogy.

Relational pedagogy 'acknowledges the matrix of human experience', rather than trying to set up false dichotomies such as child-initiated learning versus adult-led learning (Papatheodorou and Moyles 2009: 11). The focus of relational pedagogy is the 'quality encounter', which is the experience that the child has with the practitioner. This is a co-constructive process, with both child and practitioner playing a part. The role of the practitioner is to ensure that each encounter has quality and that practitioners are consciously aware of this during their time spent with the children (Papatheodorou and Moyles 2009: 185). Veale (2013: 97) states that 'co-construction of learning and knowledge-building between pedagogues and children should be aimed for'. She describes how this can be achieved through playful activities and how practitioners can then extend children's knowledge by encouraging critical thinking. The philosophy of co-construction and quality encounters are closely aligned with SST and describe the practitioner's role well.

The role of the practitioner

Rose and Rogers (2012: 2) identify the seven selves that practitioners must blend and integrate to be effective in their roles. They highlight how

PRACTICE

The power of co-construction and quality encounters

Very often planning is done 'to' children rather than with them. Even very young children can explain or demonstrate the sorts of activities they would like to do, or where they would like to play. Thornton (2002, cited in Robson 2006: 24) maintains that children need to be 'given appropriate information', but that, when this is the case 'younger children can make use of planning strategies as successfully as older children and adults'. Sustained Shared Thinking supports this pedagogy through co-constructing ideas and awareness, not just 'telling' children, but encouraging children's voices and views to be heard.

Practitioners can make this a reality by encouraging co-construction and quality encounters with children in their care. This has two additional benefits – children feel valued and supported and practitioners can be certain that their plans meet the interests of the individual child. This also highlights the role of the adult as provider of appropriate strategies. As a transferable skill, planning strategies underpin many problem-solving tasks, both in childhood and adulthood. Practitioners can nurture this skill by modelling and scaffolding this for children.

Having children either tell practitioners what they would like to play with for the day, or using photographs or Makaton pictures to illustrate their choices, can help co-construct ideas for play.

Practitioners can put small groups of children 'in charge' of areas. By listening to the children's ideas, the continuous provision can be set up to meet their interests.

Sometimes ideas for whole themes come from SST with the children, such as the child who wants to create jungle animals after seeing a DVD, which turns into a jungle area – indoors and outdoors. Sometimes it is simply one activity, such as the child who has found a ladybird outdoors and wants to recreate the spotty pattern using paint.

practitioners often face dilemmas about the types of interactions that they have with children, when it is appropriate to intervene and the nature of child-led versus child-initiated learning. They emphasise throughout that the many roles of practitioners are intertwined and complex. Of the seven selves (critical reflector, carer, communicator, facilitator, observer, assessor and creator) that Rose and Rogers identify, SST is identified in the first four. This means that SST is a vital part of being a plural practitioner.

Other theorists have described the sorts of roles that practitioners need to fulfil to be effective. For example, Veale (2013: 98) suggests that 'Practitioners need to be not only creative and enthusiastic, but also collaborative, a critical friend and provocateur'. This rings very true with SST, where collaboration, criticality and extending thought are vital aspects of SST.

In the EPPE research, Sylva *et al.* (2010: 158) identified a practitioner's good practice in the best settings. One was the role of the practitioner to 'create opportunities to extend child initiated play as well as teacher initiated group work'. This is a combination of the facilitator and creator roles identified by Rose and Rogers (2012). In addition, Sylva *et al.* state that excellent settings supported children in 'rationalising and talking through their conflicts' (Sylva *et al.* 2010: 158). This is a very beneficial use of SST, where conflicts can be talked through to both solve the conflict and also to model how children can do this for themselves as they get older and more able.

One description not yet discussed is that of 'teacher'. This can be very emotive, with some practitioners adamant that young children should not be 'taught', but that the learning comes through play, co-construction of knowledge and facilitation. The role of 'teacher' is still very connected with formal instruction, as Lindon notes about the words 'teach' and 'teaching', that they 'carry a weight of "school" meaning' (Lindon 2012b: 16). The Early Years Professional Status has been rebranded as 'Early Years Teacher', even though it doesn't currently carry Qualified Teacher Status, confusing matters even further. The EPPE definition of teaching is one of a 'full set of instructional techniques and strategies that enabled learning to take place' (Sylva *et al.* 2010: 149). Teaching, or an element of learning, whatever the term that is used, should also be part of the practitioner's role. In SST this is the shared knowledge or the 'intellectual' part of the conversation.

These show how multidimensional the role of the practitioner is. Practitioners are likely to be fulfilling several roles at any one time, and will certainly do all these things, and more, in the course of one day. Sustained Shared Thinking will support and enrich all these roles. Practitioners should try to vary their approach. For example, sometimes they are collaborators, sometimes reflector and sometimes provocateur. The modelling helps children to see different ways of approaching problems, but also helps the practitioner to see other facets of the child's personality.

PRACTICE

Practical methods for supporting SST

Professor Iram Siraj-Blatchford suggests a number of ways that practitioners can support SST with the children in their care. It is likely that you will be doing a lot of these, without even thinking about it. However, by consciously being aware of these techniques, you can ensure that you are using the full range and giving as much opportunity as possible for SST.

- Tuning in: listening carefully to what is being said, observing body language and what the child is doing.
- Showing genuine interest: giving your whole attention, maintaining eye contact, affirming, smiling, nodding.
- Respecting children's own decisions and choices.
- Inviting children to elaborate: 'I really want to know more about this'
- Re-capping: 'So you think that...'.
- Offering your own experience: 'I like to listen to music when I cook supper at home'.
- Clarifying ideas: 'Right Darren, so you think that this stone will melt if I boil it in water?'
- Suggesting: 'You might like to try doing it this way'.
- Reminding: 'Don't forget that you said that this stone will melt if I boil it'.
- Using encouragement to further thinking: 'You have really thought hard about where to put this door in the palace but where on earth will you put the windows?'
- Offering an alternative viewpoint: 'Maybe Goldilocks wasn't being naughty when she ate the porridge'.
- Speculating: 'Do you think the three bears would have liked Goldilocks to come to live with them as their friend?'
- Reciprocating: 'Thank goodness that you were wearing wellington boots when you jumped in those puddles Kwame. Look at my feet, they are soaking wet'.
- Asking open questions: 'How did you? Why does this..? What happens next? What do you think?'

> ● Modelling thinking: 'I have to think hard about what I do this evening. I need to take my dog to the vet's because he has a sore foot, take my library books back to the library and buy some food for dinner tonight. But I just won't have time to do all of these things'.
>
> (Adapted from Siraj-Blatchford 2005)

The key person

The key person role is a statutory requirement of the EYFS framework. The key person's role is described as being there to 'help ensure that every child's learning and care is tailored to meet their individual needs' (DfE 2012: 7). The role has been developed from attachment theory research, which showed that a child who forms a secure attachment with an adult has a secure emotional base from which to learn (see Chapter 3). By having one person that parents and carers and children can liaise with closely, the emotional bonds can be formed and a trusting relationship developed.

The key person, very often, meets parents and/or carers of the child at the door, takes any messages, discusses the day ahead, hands the child back at the end of the day and passes on any messages. This continuity and constancy helps to build trust and understanding between the setting and the family. These conversations can give context to the child's play. For example, if the child has spent time in the garden the previous evening, they may be keen to share their knowledge of worms or slugs with you the next day. Without context, it may be difficult to understand the child's explanation of what a worm is!

Sometimes the key person will be an active observer, but sometimes the key person must move the child's learning forward. For SST, the context can often be critical, especially for those children who are just learning to speak or for those who have speech and language difficulties. The key person can use knowledge of their key child's experiences, their intrinsic motivations and knowledge of their home life to extend conversations.

The reflective practitioner

Practitioners need to be reflective to engage thoroughly with SST. This will be both reflection 'in action' and reflection 'on action' (Schon 1983). This means either reflecting on the conversation as it is happening (in action) or reflecting

THEORY

Joint involvement episodes

In their research in 2002, Siraj-Blatchford *et al.* equate SST with Bruner's 'joint involvement episodes' (JIE). Schaffer (1996: 253) describes JIE as 'any encounter between two individuals in which the participants pay joint attention to, and jointly act upon, some external topic'. He goes on to suggest that the initiator of the interaction is usually the child, with the adult following. It is the adult's skill in using shared language, suggestions and ideas that brings the conversation onto an even footing, with both parties contributing equally. Having the skills to interact in this way was described by Dinneen as being 'highly specialised' (Dinneen 2009: 171), and certainly holds some similarities with SST. The most obvious similarities are that it is a shared encounter around a common interest and that the practitioner needs some skills to encourage and support this.

However, the difference between JIE and SST is that the JIE may only last a minute or two. The episode may simply be a child pointing out something of interest to their parent or caregiver, who responds in an interested and engaged way. In SST, this 'episode' would be extended and explored further, maybe returning to it at a later time.

The key person will have the combination of knowledge about the child's interests, context and conversation skills, to know whether to move an interaction from a JIE to a piece of Sustained Shared Thinking. Sometimes your key child may simply want to point at the rain, with no other comment needed.

afterwards (on action), possibly discussing the SST with someone else. Very often practitioners share with each other the things that children say to them. However, this is different to reflecting on the incident. Reflection includes an element of what you would or could do better next time and having a 'critical' friend can facilitate this. A critical friend is someone who will discuss your thoughts and ideas and give a reasoned evaluation. Sometimes they may be in agreement with you and at other times they may propose an alternative course of action. Both being a critical friend and having critical friendships are an important part of being a reflective practitioner.

Conclusions

The many roles of a practitioner have been discussed, as have the ways in which SST can support and enhance these roles. Most importantly, every practitioner will have their own skill set, built from their own experiences, knowledge, culture, beliefs and values. Inevitably this will, and should, have some impact on your interactions with children. You may approach SST in a very different way to your colleague. This could be very beneficial for the children in your care, as children will react differently to different approaches. By having a range of different approaches the children will benefit from observing how people are different and will also be able to try different forms of SST for themselves.

The relationship between the child and the practitioner, adult or parent plays an important part in establishing SST. This is likely to be an established relationship, where the adult can tune in quickly and easily to the child's interests, thought process and context. Similarly, the child can communicate readily with the adult, whether this is verbal or non-verbal communication.

As well as the relationship between the two people involved with the SST, practitioners should also consider whether they understand the subject area that is interesting to the child. For example, would it be better for someone who understands plants to do the SST outdoors? A practitioner who only has basic knowledge may not be able to stretch and challenge the children as effectively as someone who has in-depth knowledge.

6 Environments to support Sustained Shared Thinking

A rich environment for play is a vital source of child-initiated, sustained, shared thinking opportunities that watchful, sensitive adults can pick up on.

(Glazzard et al. 2010: 74)

Introduction

This chapter investigates the sorts of environments, physical and emotional, that support SST. The discussion about the physical environment starts with Communication Friendly Spaces (Jarman 2012) and then expands to look at a range of environments and areas that could be used to support SST. This includes practical ideas for setting up 'classic' areas, such as the sand and water trays, so that SST can happen naturally. The discussion about the emotional environment starts with some theory around self-esteem and self-confidence in young children and how this can be fostered (Dowling 2010). This then moves onto the practitioner's emotional wellbeing (DCSF 2008b) and how an emotionally secure environment is important when supporting children.

This chapter also explores the 'whole' environment of the setting, whether this is a nursery, school or childminder, with regards to the overall ethos.

Physical environment

Jarman (2012: 1) states that 'it is critical to understand how the physical space should connect with the underpinning pedagogy of the setting'. One of the most common questions asked about SST is how this can be achieved in a busy nursery setting, or when you are in a room with children of different ages to consider, or in managing a busy classroom. Often SST would be most easily done on a one-to-one basis in a quiet area, where you can give the child your full, undivided attention. However, in real settings this is unlikely to be the case. This will mean that you will have to think more carefully about how the physical environment is set up. Rose and Rogers (2012) discuss four different types of environments that practitioners may encounter in a setting:

1. prohibiting environment;
2. affording environment;
3. inviting environment;
4. potentiating environment.

These environments are listed in order of support for SST. So the prohibiting environment has little support for SST, whereas the potentiating environment has plenty of opportunities for children to be involved with SST. It is important that practitioners audit their environments to ensure that they do not prohibit SST. For example, that quiet areas, such as a corner separated off, are created or that the equipment is not set out so that it encourages children to run up and down the room. At the very least the environment should be inviting and welcoming so children want to come to join adults and talk to them, whether this is at the play dough table or in the home corner. This means having practitioners down at the child's level (not stood over them), ready to engage with the children and having welcoming body language (a smile).

With babies and young children, the environment is more likely to be peaceful than with the more physically able and active pre-schoolers. This will give practitioners working with babies more opportunities to find those quiet one-to-one moments. This could be when other children are asleep or when you are changing nappies, for example. These do not need to be 'planned' but practitioners need to be aware that, when they do get these opportunities, to make the most of them.

It is good practice to have a quiet area for toddlers, which they can access independently. This enables them to reflect on the day's experiences, relax and have time to absorb all the information that is around them. The area can simply be hung with a curtain or piece of fabric (removable if necessary for alarm systems) and furnished with a few large scatter cushions. The children really enjoy these areas if they feel that the adults can't see them. You can achieve this by having reasonably high barriers around the area, which the children can hide behind, but that practitioners can see over the top of. These areas may also be used for quiet 'withdraw' areas so adults can engage in SST with individual children or small groups of children. These are also good places to encourage children to talk to each other and engage in peer learning, especially if you have children of different ages together. Similarly, it is beneficial for pre-schoolers to have a quiet area outdoors as well, such as a thinking bench, secret garden or den (Jarman 2009). This could simply be a small corner or triangle of the garden that is out of the way and 'belongs' to the children. To make this even more special, the practitioners are only allowed in with the express permission of the children.

However, the environment does not have to be quiet or empty to have extended periods of SST. Practitioners can still have conversations that solve problems or stretch thinking in the middle of the busiest classroom or in the outdoor environment. In fact, many of the problem-solving aspects of SST will be in the midst of complex and active play. For example, it may be that the children would like to mix different coloured paints to get a desired colour, but are unsure how to do this. The practitioner can discuss how to solve this problem and also introduce some ideas about change, mixing and paint as media mark making, during a busy craft activity. For SST outdoors, the children may find mini-beasts under a log and want to know all about their habitat and names. This is an ideal time to discuss with the children where these creatures have come from, why they live in the dark and the sorts of things they may eat.

For older children it may be advantageous for practitioners to have planned quieter periods at certain points throughout the day. These may occur naturally like, for example, after teatime, when children first return from their lunchtime play, or it could be a brief time during the day when all the practitioners work with their key group of children. Practitioners may also plan for quieter periods, such as a circle time or story time, when children can be encouraged and supported to share their thoughts. As with all planning, this should be flexible and follow the children's interests, being adapted as necessary.

PRACTICE

Most settings have defined areas, such as the water play area, sand tray, construction, etc. Very often, during a busy day, it can be difficult to think of questions to promote SST in a particular area. One idea is to have a discrete card or notice that has a number of suggested questions for practitioners to use in that particular area or to support play in general. For example:

- 'What happens if you get the sand wet?'
- 'How could we make the bubbles bigger?'
- 'Which shaped block would fit in here?'

If there are any questions that practitioners find that are particularly good for stimulating conversation, they can add these to the bottom of the card for others to use.

In addition, you could have suggestions for enhancing the continuous provision, such as adding coloured ice-cubes to the water tray. These ideas can be discussed with the children beforehand, to see what they think may happen (float/sink, what will happen to the colour?) and then tested out for real.

Take photos of construction in the construction area, to display and to remind both practitioners and children of previous achievements. The SST can be around whether the constructions can be replicated or improved.

The book area is a natural place for SST, as it tends to be furnished with soft cushions and in a quiet area. However, the SST does not always have to be about books. You can use books and images to start conversations about family, pets, celebrations, getting to the setting – anything that inspires your child.

Social environment

The complex and interwoven social environment will have an impact on a child's development. Bronfenbrenner (1979) described how there may be different impacts, depending on the type of interactions (see the Theory box below). Nurseries and other settings, such as childminders, nannies and au pairs, may have a significant influence on the social ecological system, which will occur in the meso-system. For SST this means that the parents and carers have the most significant effect, so good practice needs to be reinforced in the home learning environment.

The social environment that is fostered at the setting is important for SST. In practice this will mean encouraging older children to discuss their ideas and interests with each other. Practitioners will need to model this for toddlers, either between adults or using a running narrative to demonstrate how the children can have a two-way conversation. Encouraging friendships such as these supports social development and also 'helps children to feel positive about themselves and others' (DCSF 2008c: card 2.1).

THEORY

Bronfenbrenner: *The Ecology of Human Development*

Urie Bronfenbrenner proposed and developed the Ecological Systems Theories of child development (Bronfenbrenner 1979). In its simplest form, this theory postulates that a child will develop within many layers of social interactions. The layers are nested one within another, just as an onion has layers of skin, with the child at the very centre.

The closer the layer is to the child at the centre, the more influence that layer will have on the child's development. Thus the closest layer – direct family, including parents, carers and siblings – will have the most influence on the child. The furthest layer, which includes the global community and cultural landscape, will have a lesser effect. Not only will the closest layers have the most effect on the child's development, but the child is also able to co-construct and affect these interactions more than any of the others.

Bronfenbrenner identified five ecological systems:

1. microsystem – the innermost layer: child's immediate family;
2. mesosystem – second layer: extended family, school and immediate community;
3. exosystem – third layer: employment status of parents, availability of libraries;
4. macrosystem – fourth layer: cultural landscape and demographic of the child's life;
5. chronosystem – fifth layer: time (this encompasses all other layers and acknowledges that there will be changes over time, with children growing up, new siblings, changes in schools, etc.).

Further reading

Bronfenbrenner, U. (2005) *Making Human Beings Human: Bioecological Perspectives on Human Development* London: Sage.

This is a retrospective collection of 23 articles written or co-authored by Bronfenbrenner, which shows his ideas and theories unfolding over 60 years. This book is an absorbing insight into his thoughts and work.

▉ Emotional environment

The emotional environment is how the setting makes the children 'feel'. It should be welcoming, inclusive and respectful. Practitioners can achieve this through the physical environment, by displaying pictures of the children, having meaningful cultural artefacts and providing children with their own pegs or places to leave their possessions. The practitioners themselves provide the majority of the emotional environment. This is closely allied with the key person approach, as described in Chapter 5, and is centred on 'close, warm and supportive' relationships (DCSF 2008c: card 1.4).

Sustained Shared Thinking supports a positive emotional environment by recognising respectful discussions as being part of the normal routine of the setting. For babies and younger children this may be as simple as a word of praise or a delighted expression at something they have achieved. For older children this could be a sustained discussion about a problem or achievement. A child's self-esteem and a sense of wellbeing can be fostered by recognising and valuing children's contributions. This is particularly important when talking about feelings, and giving toddlers the words to express their emotions.

The original EYFS (DCSF 2008c: card 3.3) states that 'when children feel confident in the environment they are willing to try things out, knowing that their effort is valued'.

▓ Practitioner approaches to the environment

The practitioner's approach to the environment can make the difference between the setting working, with full engagement and high levels of involvement, and the children being bored. Just as each child is unique, each practitioner is unique, so each practitioner will approach any environment in a different way. One practitioner may see an obstacle course as an opportunity for 'rough and tumble' play, whereas another may see the same obstacle course as an opportunity for concentration and problem solving. Therefore, the practitioners using the environment should understand what is trying to be achieved with each activity. This may require a formal training or teaching session, to ensure that everyone can make the most of the opportunities being offered. Alternatively, practitioners can share their ideas when setting up the activity, with a brief explanation of what they are hoping to achieve by it, especially if the activity is to meet the specific interests of a particular child.

Reflection

As a child, I think I must have had an enclosure schema. I like to put away things in boxes, sitting in the corner at cafes and naturally draw boxes around notes when writing. When going into settings, I'm drawn to the tents and hideaway corners. In one setting that I visit regularly there is a triangular piece of the garden that is hidden behind a large tree. The owner of the setting could have fenced this piece off or banned the children from playing in this area because they're partially hidden from view. However, she has chosen to let the children have this as their very own area. No adults are allowed in, unless given express permission.

I really like this area, partially because it speaks to my enclosure schema, but mainly because whenever I visit there are always two or three children hidden away in this little spot having deep and meaningful conversations. These conversations may be about anything, from what they ate at lunchtime to the latest superhero. This is such a natural thing for children to do, that you do not have persuade or encourage children in their SST with each other.

When, as an adult, I have been invited into the special area, I have felt particularly privileged and have felt that the SST that I have had while in the children's own area is especially magical.

In the particular case of SST, every practitioner, whatever their level of qualification, should be able to identify and capitalise on opportunities wherever they occur.

▓ Play – what is the role of play in SST?

Play is notoriously difficult to define. Dubiel (2012) suggests that the defining principle of play is that it is child-initiated, that the child has ownership of the project or the challenge, and that the child has chosen to do it. Chilvers (2012: 1) notes that 'there is something wonderful about the way in which children are born to play'. She suggests that practitioners take time to consider the types of play that children can access at the setting and whether they are motivated and excited in their play. Angela Anning, in Moyles (2010: 30) suggests that practitioners should adopt 'spontaneous playful interactions and dialogue with children in episodes such as functional play and games with rules' in order to support a pedagogy of play. All of these descriptions and definitions fit well with both the methods and ideology of SST. Play and SST work well together and practitioners should be aware that SST can support play, by extending it, making it more playful or just encouraging children to do what they do naturally.

Children explore concepts and ideas through their play. Vygotsky (1978), while discussing rules in play, analysed Sully's observation of two sisters, who chose to play a game of 'sisters'. This can often be seen in younger children, where the mum is expected to play the part of 'mummy'. In this way children are exploring their own ideas of how certain roles are fulfilled by different types of people. The element of SST heightens and complicates this type of play, as rules become more complex and interwoven. He also goes on to describe how pre-school children start to turn the concrete situation around. Instead of needing to have the real object to interact with, other objects are substituted to represent the toy, such as a stick being a horse. This is quite high-level thinking for children and practitioners can start to see where a child's thinking is at by observing this sort of play. By engaging in SST, the meaning and significance of the representational object can be discussed.

At the pre-school age, children can start to differentiate between the meanings of words, even if the visual clues are contrary to what they are saying. As children get older, they move away from having to have objects, to games, rules, imagination, being beyond themselves. SST supports, encourages and models this, just as physical toys and objects and pictures do for younger children.

Older children verbalise, so we can hear and see their activities. Younger children have to be observed through their actions alone. Just as adults, we 'bounce ideas' off each other, usually coming to a deeper understanding or clearer vision of our own ideas, so children share their ideas and concepts, testing them against those of others.

Sustained Shared Thinking is not unique to child-initiated play and could just as easily occur during adult-led or adult-supported play. If you have 'small group' time or a period of time with your key children, you could plan to have some SST with the group. This will enable you to think about some questions and ideas that you may wish to investigate. It also allows you to prepare any materials for later work such as, for example, getting out the dressing up box if you are going to be talking about role play.

■ The whole environment and ethos of the setting

Tickell (2011: 97) explains the distinction between the Prime and Specific Areas of learning and development in the EYFS. Although this is applied to the EYFS, the theory also holds for other curricula (such as the Curriculum for Excellence in Scotland, the Foundation Phase for Wales and the Foundation Stage for Northern Ireland).

The Prime Areas of learning and development

'Experience expectant learning' is the learning that babies are genetically primed to receive. This includes basic stimulus (touch, sight, auditory) that will inform the brain of the environment. It also includes the interactions between parents and carers and baby. The Prime Areas of the EYFS fall under experience expectant learning. Thus personal, social and emotional development (PSED), physical development (PD) and communication and language (CL) are Prime Areas. As we learn more from neuroscience, we are beginning to understand how this learning occurs and its nuances. For example, although there is evidence for language development having 'sensitive periods' (Hall 2005: 16) this is not the whole story. There appear to be sensitive periods for sensory and motor development as well. However, the adage of 'use it or lose it' for synapsis development is exaggerated (so it is never too late to learn something new!). What appears to be more important is that any impairment needs to be identified and worked on as soon as possible. 'The sooner remediation of any deficit begins, the greater chance there is of overcoming the deficit' (Hall 2005: 21).

The Specific Areas of learning and development

The Specific Areas of learning and development under the EYFS are more culturally dependent and are not essential to basic survival. For example, speech is essential to communicate needs and wants, at an early age. However, people can survive without being able to read or write or understand mathematics. This is not to say that these things are not desirable – they are in modern society and in Western culture. They are just not essential for survival, as thriving physically is. These areas of learning are called 'experience dependent' because they will only occur if there is a need for it culturally and socially (Tickell 2011: 97). They can be thought of as 'cultural tools for thinking' and include writing, numbers and maps. It should be noted that these tools will change over time as society and cultures change. For example, I have spent many hours teaching children how to use a mouse for a computer, accurate clicking and right/left hand buttons. With the advent of touch screens (everything from phones to watches to computers) this is going to be a largely redundant skill in the future.

The project approach

Sargent (2011a: 3) promotes the project approach, as these 'provide an ideal arena for promoting thinking skills'. Katz and Chard (2000: 5) define a project as something where 'children's ideas, questions, theories, predictions and interests are major determinants of the experiences provided'. Therefore, the children themselves steer the project, where their ideas have come from SST. This has two advantages:

1. the children will be engaged in activities that they are interested in because they have instigated and evolved these ideas;
2. the practitioner can see the development of the children's thought processes and learning as the project develops.

Recording SST

Sustained Shared Thinking, by its very nature, is about process, not product, and is very fleeting. There are a number of reasons why practitioners would want to record SST.

1. To revisit and recall with the children. It is really useful to record (even in note form) what you have discussed, so you can return to the conversation, if appropriate. You could keep artefacts and photos as well.

2. To feedback to parents. In the busyness of the day, it can be very easy to forget who you have spoken to and about what. Invariably your mind goes blank when there is a parent standing in front of you! Keeping a note can just jog your memory to recall the conversation to share with parents.

3. To display for everyone to enjoy. Really good displays will include work from the children, photos during the activity and 'speech bubbles' that contain comments from the children. This supports children's self-esteem because they can see that both the product (picture, etc.) *and* their words are valued by the practitioners. Practitioners should make sure to read out the words for the children and remind them of saying them.

4. Evidence. This could be for Early Years Teacher Status, internal audit purposes or Ofsted. In this case, the SST may need to be recorded verbatim. If you know you will have to use the SST for this purpose, it is worth getting permissions to record the conversation, so you have time to transcribe it back afterwards.

It is definitely more important to 'be in the moment' with your child, rather than worrying about remembering the conversation afterwards. Children are very good at picking up on someone who is not really fully listening. However, if you need a record, you could ask another practitioner just to make a quick note while you finish the conversation or have a pen and pad to hand so you can record the SST as soon as possible.

▮ Conclusions

The physical and emotional environments both play a part in a child's development and should be considered equally. It is worth auditing your environment to see if there are any gaps or anything that practitioners are not sure about. Play, and a play-based environment, is very important for children. Sustained Shared Thinking can support the environment and help enrich it, by including the thoughts and ideas of the children. Practitioners should think about how they might record SST and display this for the children, so that they know that their words and views are valued.

Further reading

Salmon and Lucas (2011) have produced a very interesting journal article about how children think and make the thinking visible: Salmon, A. and Lucas, T. (2011) 'Exploring Young Children's Conceptions about Thinking'. *Journal of Research in Childhood Education* Vol. 25, Iss 4 pp. 364–375.

Different ages, different requirements, including SEN

But it is extremely important to recognise that the pedagogic form that 'Sustained Shared Thinking' takes with children under age two is quite different from that most appropriate for three to five year olds.

(Siraj-Blatchford 2007: 1)

Introduction

This chapter looks at how SST is different for children of different ages. The focus is on practical ideas for suitable activities, across three broad age ranges: babies, toddlers and pre-schoolers. Sharing thoughts and ideas with pre-school aged children is going to be very different to SST with babies or children who are pre-speech. This is not to say that it is impossible, but that it requires different skills, abilities and thought process.

This chapter also discusses some of the things that practitioners may need to consider if they have children with Special Educational Needs (SEN).

Different ages, different requirements

Initiating SST with children of different ages needs different skills from practitioners, just as children need a different approach. The older children in the setting are more likely to approach you, asking to know your name and what you are doing (especially if you have a pen and pad to hand!). Some toddlers may be more hesitant, seeking assurances from their key person or friends that it is all right to speak to this particular adult. A baby is unlikely to engage in an extended engagement with anyone other than his or her key person or close family member. Siraj-Blatchford (2007: 1) explains how children's play is an ever-shifting continuum that gradually develops over time. This will affect the way children are gradually influenced more by their peers than the adults in their life.

Allowing time for children to absorb the information is as important as giving them stimulating environments. The research from neuroscience is showing that a baby's brain can be just as active when asleep as when they are awake (Oates *et al.* 2012). The amount of time that you allow for a pre-schooler to absorb an idea is going to be far less than the amount of time you would allow for a toddler. You should also always remember that toddlers are seeing most things for the first time, while pre-schoolers may have already come across the concept or seen the idea before.

Age ranges

The age ranges suggested here are broad outlines to demonstrate how SST may look different throughout early childhood. Children all develop at different rates and every child will interact in a unique way. This means that the practitioner should be aware of their child's level of ability and the level of support that will stretch and challenge without setting the child up for failure. When discussing how play, and particularly 'pretend' play, develops, Siraj-Blatchford suggests that there is a difference in the adult's role, depending on the age of the child, with practitioner support being 'paramount before the age of two years, while peer play may be more significant around age four' (Siraj-Blatchford, 2009: 7). Most practitioners will automatically, without noticing, adapt their interactions with children of different ages and abilities. This is worth modeling or discussing with less-experienced practitioners, so they notice the subtle changes. For example, using short sentences, supported with gestures are more appropriate for younger children. It is no good trying to have a developmentally inappropriate, in-depth conversation with a child. Making some small changes, such as using objects of reference or a picture book, may mean a more successful piece of SST.

Babies

Sustained Shared Thinking is closely tied to speech and language. However, it is entirely possible to solve a problem and to exchange ideas with a baby, even before they can talk. The skill is to adapt the practitioner's viewpoint to understand how to communicate effectively with babies. Gopnik (2009: 2) explains how 'babies' intelligence, the research shows, is very different from that of adults and from the kind of intelligence we usually cultivate in schools'. At school the work is designed to meet a learning outcome, an aim, a specific learning point, whereas babies are more likely to explore many different outcomes. Gopnik (2009: 3) likens this to the computer scientist, who defines the difference between exploring and exploiting as: 'a system will learn more if it explores many possibilities, but it will be more effective if it simply acts on the most likely one. Babies explore; adults exploit'.

As practitioners we should be encouraging babies to explore, not prune their creativity and thoughts to 'exploit' their ideas and rush them to the 'correct' solution every time. There are a few occasions where the 'correct' solution may be important. For example, that the oven will be hot when in use or not to pull the cat's tail. However, there are many more opportunities to explore the world with your baby or young child before they have to use their spotlight thinking and concentrate on one area. Veale (2013) explains how some practitioners may underestimate the communication abilities of a baby and may feel that SST with babies is a waste of time or not worthwhile for the baby. However, this is far from the truth and more research is indicating just how able babies actually are.

THEORY

Babies communicate in many ways, including crying, moving and facial expressions. Dowling (2013: 19) asserts that 'babies use body language, eye contact and gesture' and that 'their questions are clearly conveyed when they point to an object and confront the adult with a searching look'. As a practitioner, you will need to cue into these and encourage the protoconversations that will occur. A protoconversation is the two-way interaction between adult and baby, where each takes a turn at verbalising (which may be baby babbling or motherese for the adult). There is research to show that 'sensitivity to speech sounds begins prenatally, and newborns already show some remarkable capacities related to language' (Oates et al. 2012: 44).

While researching intersubjectivity (a shared meaning or understanding between two people) Trevarthen (2011: 121) found that babies 'are born with motives and emotions for actions that sustain human intersubjectitivity'. That is to say that even a very young baby seems to be pre-programmed to try to keep another human's interest. He described how babies might use many different methods (body movement, facial expressions) to share meanings and intentions. He also suggests that babies will do this on purpose, to provoke a response. This research demonstrates that, even before they can talk, babies are ready to engage in SST and already have body movements and facial expressions to help them.

Further reading

There is always more research about babies and their reactions. This piece of research is particularly interesting. The team from University of London,

University College London and Kings College London have investigated the 'atypical social interactions [that] are characteristic' of autism – but in the first six months of a baby's life. They found that there were 'specific differences in localizable brain function within the first 6 months of life in a group of infants at risk for autism. Further, these differences closely resemble known patterns of neural atypicality in children and adults with autism'. The suggestion is that autism could be diagnosed in babies as young as six months.

Lloyd-Fox S., Blasi A., Elwell C., Charman T., Murphy D. and Johnson M. (2013) 'Reduced neural sensitivity to social stimuli in infants at risk for autism'. *Proceedings of the Royal Society B* 280: 20123026. Available from: http://www.cbcd.bbk.ac.uk/people/scientificstaff/sarah_f/Lloyd-Fox-PRSoc%20article%202013.pdf (last accessed 26 October 2013).

There is more research to be published in this area and it will be fascinating to see how this develops.

For some babies SST should be started with physical contact, such as the stroking of an arm, so you 'cue' them into the interaction and have their full attention. Babies may have a very short engagement time and it is dependent on the baby feeling safe, secure and physically comfortable. Sustained Shared Thinking may be observed as prolonged gazing or watching intently from the baby, as well as positive body language, while the adult's role is to give encouragement, reassurance and praise.

It is important for the practitioner to be able to see the baby's face clearly, but at the right distance so that the baby can also see the practitioner. The SST may be a series of vocalisations that happen between baby and practitioner, equivalent to extending a narrative. It could also be the practitioner 'solving the problem' of a toy being repeatedly thrown from the high chair. In this case, the practitioner would make a comment or facial expression to show how the toy has been found – 'Here it is!' – so the baby makes the connection.

The environment for SST with babies is particularly important. The room or environment needs to be relatively distraction free and calm. The baby should be relaxed and comfortable. It is worth checking the noise levels, both indoors and outdoors, for background noise that, as adults, we filter out subconsciously. Even the whirring of a fan or the drone of a tractor in the distance may be too distracting for a baby to concentrate fully. Be realistic about the amount of time that a baby will concentrate for. It is likely to only be a few minutes, if that. However, if you do find an interaction that your baby enjoys, it could be a lot longer.

Toddlers

Toddlers are just finding their independence and personalities. They may have a few words, or a larger vocabulary. Many toddlers will be fascinated with the world around them and be actively engaged with 'problem solving', such as how to open cupboards, how to climb up the bookshelf and yoghurt as a painting material. Sustained Shared Thinking can be used to harness this natural curiosity, to discuss or physically explore 'what might happen if...'.

Toddlers will also go through the 'Why?' stage, where every utterance will start with 'Why...?'. This can be a massive advantage when considering SST, because it is a natural way to start exploring a concept. It is interesting to note that most toddlers will want a 'proper' explanation that makes sense to them. This was shown by Frazier *et al.* (2009), who found from two longitudinal studies of children aged two to four that children were more satisfied when they received an explanation than when they did not. This shows how children of this age are the most eager to have SST, because they want to have the in-depth, explanatory conversations that characterise SST.

Engaging toddlers may be the easiest, because of their natural curiosity. Once engaged in a conversation, the practitioner's skill is to follow the child's interest, to solve the problem, clarify a concept or evaluate activities.

If it is difficult to understand toddlers or children who are just learning to speak, you can always 'go with the flow'. If you keep asking a toddler to repeat a word or idea, they will soon lose interest and wander off. Quiet toddlers may watch to catch your eye, checking out to see if you are interested in them. Practitioners should watch out for these opportunities and gauge whether the toddler is ready to engage in SST or not. Do not be anxious if the toddler doesn't want to engage right away – it may take several encounters before they are secure enough to engage with you.

There is a massive difference between toddlers and babies. If you are working with the children all the time, you may not notice the change which takes place gradually. It is worthwhile stopping every so often and reviewing their stage of development to ensure that you are keeping up with them. This could be increasing the complexity of your sentence structure, extending vocabulary choices or introducing more difficult concepts.

THEORY

At around 18 months, toddlers will start to put two words together – 'teddy gone' – but will be able to understand much more of what you say to them. They will be able to understand simple instructions and have an ever-increasing vocabulary.

Between 12 months and 24 months, the number of words that a child knows is likely to increase from around 10 to over 300. Between the ages of two and three, toddlers will start to link four or five words together.

This rate of progress in talking and understanding language is astounding and varies considerably from child to child.

Further reading

For more information about speech and language, including whom to contact if you have concerns, visit: www.ican.org.uk

Pre-school

Pre-school children tend to be more confident talkers and will engage in conversations with both adults and children of all ages. Practitioners can use the full range of SST with this age range and will usually get a positive response. Practitioners should also be aware that there will be some good SST going on between children, and to be sure to record this, only interfering if necessary. The essential aspect is that children are engaging in SST, encouraging critical thinking and creativity.

Pre-school children usually have a range of different play and interactions, both with adults and other children. Some different ways that they engage in SST are:

● starting conversations with unfamiliar adults;
● self talking and talking out loud to explain their motivation for play;
● negotiating with other children, either to join the play or to persuade someone to join their play; this can sometimes be very sophisticated, with reasoned arguments and compensation involved;
● some children at this age are beginning to play with language, enjoy telling each other jokes (often explaining them as well) and making up words;
● testing out ideas with other children to see what their ideas are such as, for example, explaining where the climbing frame would be best placed because of the sand pit and the football game – solving these sorts of problems can get very involved indeed!

THEORY

Children develop ways of thinking differently to those of adults. In their excellent book *How Children Develop*, Siegler *et al.* discuss some of the strategies that children use. They found that:

1. children use a variety of ways of thinking – not just one;
2. children use diverse strategies that last over a long period;
3. children experiment until they find the most reliable or successful strategies, which they finally rely on.

(Adapted from Siegler et al. 2010)

Practitioners should be aware of this and adapt their approaches to SST as children grow older and begin to find their most reliable strategies. In practice this can be very frustrating, as you think that a child has understood a concept, just to find that they haven't. For example, having done lots of ice cubes in the water tray, talking about melting and water and ice, I felt sure that my pre-school child understood this concept. The next day, when the puddles were frozen, he didn't make the connection between 'outdoor ice' and 'indoor ice' and was amazed when the puddle melted to water.

Special Educational Needs

Special Educational Needs (SEN) covers a massive spectrum of socially constructed issues and medical diagnoses. Just as you cannot pigeonhole all children of the same age together; you cannot group all children with SEN together. If you consider that most children will have glue ear at some time, and therefore intermittent hearing, then most children will need additional support for hearing impairment at some time.

In this section are some thoughts about children with SEN and how to support them with SST. When considering children with SEN, practitioners should include Gifted and Talented children, because these children will also need additional support with more challenging and stretching activities.

For children with SEN, SST is based on careful observation, especially if children can't communicate verbally or can't communicate their ideas at all. Practitioners should also be aware that some children with SEN might be more adept at problem solving than others because they are doing it all the time. For example, getting up and down steps while using a walker. They might also be good at picking up cues from other children about what is going on. For example, children who have a hearing impairment (permanent or otherwise) may not be able to hear the 'tidy up' song, but can guess from the reaction of the other children as to what is required of them.

PRACTICE

Thinking about observations

One observation technique that is used to identify triggers or situations that may influence behaviour is the STAR approach. This is particularly useful for children who may be on the autistic spectrum, where triggers may be very small or unpredictable.

- S is for setting. Whereabouts did the challenging behaviour or dispute occur? Be as specific as possible because the exact location may be important. For example, if it was under a tree outdoors, it may be that something fell or it may be near a flashing light indoors.
- T is for trigger. What was it that triggered the behaviour? Was it another child, adult, noise, change in light?
- A is for action. What actually happened?
- R is for response. What was your response? Was it proportionate and reasonable? Check that you are not rewarding challenging behaviour.

The STAR approach to observations will help to inform you of the child's interests, and also of the sorts of stimuli that you may wish to avoid. It may be fun for you to play with gloop, but it could be torture for a child who has a sensory processing disorder.

You can still engage in SST with children who have speech complications, such as selective mutism (phobia of talking) or those with unusual speech patterns (some children with autism). Practitioners can still solve problems together with children, such as how to build a high tower with the bricks, and explore concepts, such as a pulley system. The difference will be that the practitioner may have to have a running commentary to model and facilitate the activity. Of course, working together to solve a problem may not require any words at all, just cooperation and collaboration.

Reflection

Over the years I have worked with many children who have speech and language difficulties. This is not unusual; most practitioners will come across children who have speech, language and communication difficulties as a regular part of their daily work. This can make SST more complicated and possibly more frustrating, for both adult and child.

One young boy, who was my key child, had particular difficulty with most aspects of his speech. However, he was a very determined boy who did not let the fact that his speech was indistinct stop him communicating his thoughts to me. One day he was getting very frustrated because I could not understand what he was trying to tell me. I had asked him several questions, to try and establish the context of the question, so I could try to guess what the matter was. I knew it was something about me, because he kept pointing at me. I had also established that he wanted to play something with me. Finally, he gave up and walked off. I felt a little disappointed that I'd not been able to work it out, when he returned with the sign from the wall, which illustrated my good listening rules. These were centred on good sitting, good listening and good-looking. This was what he had been trying to tell me to do in order to play the game with him. Because I had not been able to work it out for myself, he had chosen to help me by using a visual aid.

In that moment I realised that I could have done the same for him, and communicated non-verbally, with pictures or with objects of reference. His ability to sustain the conversation and solve the problem had far exceeded my own. This has often given me pause for thought when considering children who have additional needs. It is better to listen to their conversations than it is to impose your own upon them.

In the current EYFS Profile (2012), children are either exceeding (beyond the level of development expected at the end of the EYFS), expected (at the level expected) or emerging (not yet at the level expected) (DfE 2013: 11). Use of the word 'emerging' suggests that at some point they will achieve this stage, and that they are currently achieving 'less than expected'. For some children with SEN this becomes a problem, because some children will never reach 'the level expected' for their age and these skills will never 'emerge'.

THEORY

Different forms of communication – communicating through sign language

BSL

Sign language is a way of communicating used by over 50,000 people in the UK (BSL 2013) and is used by people who have a hearing impairment or who are deaf. It is a way of communicating using your hands, facial expressions and body language.

Each country has its own version of sign language, with the one in the UK being called British Sign Language (BSL). There are variations between each signed language. For example, American Sign Language only uses one hand to sign out the letters of the alphabet, while BSL uses two hands in conjunction with each other. There are even variations within each sign language, so someone in the North of the UK may use a different BSL sign for objects to someone in the South. This is equivalent to regional dialects in a spoken language. However, there is enough commonality for people to make themselves understood throughout the UK.

BSL has its own syntax, which reduces the number of words that need to be signed, without losing the meaning. For example, rather than signing 'What is your name?' the BSL sign equivalent is 'Your name what?' The meaning can be understood, but the extraneous 'is' does not need to be signed.

SSE

Sign Supported English (SSE) uses the syntax and word order of spoken English, but is supported with the signs of BSL. For example, in 'What is your name?' every word would be signed and in that order. Sign Supported English is useful for children who are either not ready or are unable to learn the more complex syntax of BSL. It is also useful for times when there are both hearing and Deaf children present.

Makaton

The word 'Makaton' comes from a combination of the inventors' names – Ma for Margaret, Ka for Katherine and Ton for Tony (ELCE 2013). Makaton also uses hands and facial expressions, but it combines these with symbols and some speech. It is not a true 'language' in that it is supported with verbal communication and follows English syntax. It is used to support children who have a range of SEN, rather than just hearing impairments. There is a core vocabulary, which has both hand signs and visual images to illustrate and reinforce the concepts being discussed. The signs are based on BSL signs.

The Makaton symbols can convey the meanings independent of the sign and are usually very simple, stylised black line drawings on a white background.

You can find some examples of signs at the Makaton charity website: http://www.makaton.org/shop/shopping/browseStore/Free-resources. They even update them with seasonal signs. These can be used to support nursery rhymes, songs and stories, or they can be used to create time lines, box labels, lists, etc.

PRACTICE

Practical equipment to support communication

There are many pieces of equipment that can help give children a 'voice'. These may be children with SEN, but could equally be shy children or those who are temporarily struggling to communicate due to reasons beyond their control. Children will feel more included and able to share their interests by using these pieces of equipment, as well as being more able to sustain thinking.

'BIGmack' switches to give the child a voice

These are recording devices that can store around two minutes of speech or sounds. They can be used as a setting/home diary or your child can record a response like, for example, a refrain in a story to use at circle time.

Switch adaptors

There are adapters that can plug into toys that require children to press buttons. These allow children with limited mobility or visual impairments to use the toys, helping integration.

Puppets

Puppets can be very useful for children who are shy or who have limited social development. Very often children will happily chat to a puppet because there are no expectations or pressure on them to give the 'right' answer, especially if the puppet is shy as well! Sargent (2011b) explains how photographs of puppets doing risky or 'naughty' things are good for starting and promoting SST.

Conclusions

Sustained Shared Thinking will look very different between a baby and a practitioner and a pre-school child and a practitioner. Both are valuable for the child and support different parts of the child's developmental needs.

Babies need to have close contact, good eye contact and a calm, relaxed atmosphere to get the very best out of SST. Toddlers are more likely to lead the conversations, particularly with the question 'Why?' and practitioners need to be skilled at giving informative answers. Pre-school children have usually developed a range of strategies that means they can enjoy SST with familiar adults and other children. Some children will be very skilful at using SST to make sense of the world around them.

Further reading

Gopnik, A. (2011) *What do babies think?* Available from: http://www.ted.com/talks/alison_gopnik_what_do_babies_think.html (last accessed on 10 July 2013).

In this 15-minute TED lecture, Professor Gopnik discusses what babies are thinking, how we can learn from this and what we need to do to support it.

8 Parents, carers and the home learning environment

> The evidence is unequivocal that working in partnership with families
> to build on the learning that goes on in the home is the best way to
> have an effective impact on the development of children.
>
> (Whalley and Arnold 2013)

Introduction

This chapter considers SST from a different viewpoint – that of the parents and carers. The home learning environment (HLE) has been shown to have a 'significant positive impact' on a child's development (Sylva *et al.* 2004), so it is essential to ensure that SST is supported both at home and in the setting. Here we explore how settings can communicate the importance of SST to parents and carers. Some of the different sorts of activities that can be shared by the setting with parents and carers are discussed.

One of the first things to consider is that parents and carers, just as children, are not a homogenous group. The parents and carers who you will come across at your settings will be as individual and unique as the children are. This means that they will have a variety of concerns, skills, changing family situations, dispositions and backgrounds. Therefore the support and interactions you will have with the family will vary, and your interactions will probably vary from week to week with the same family as situations change. For example, the family dynamics will change if mum has a new baby.

Here, some of the broader aspects of working with parents and carers are considered. It is almost impossible to discuss everything that you may come across as a practitioner. However, if you always try to consider the situation from the parents' and carers' point of view, you are more likely to meet their needs.

■ Home learning environment

The HLE is more than just the place that the child calls home. Although an all-encompassing definition of the HLE is difficult, it is generally agreed that it is 'an interaction between parent and child in a way that enables the child to learn' (Hunt *et al.* 2011: 5). It also consists of the types of activities that children and their parents or carers are involved in at home and the emotional environment. For example, this may include reading together, singing nursery rhymes, going on visits to such places as the library or the park, having friends to play and playing with numbers.

Reflection

Very often children are more than happy to talk about their home-learning experiences. This is particularly true when talking about pets, family members or special occasions.

Harry is around 2 ½ years' old and attends nursery regularly. He is a confident little lad who has many interests. The following dialogue occurred between Harry and myself at nursery. It is all the more remarkable because I had only just met Harry.

Me: 'Hello, my name is Kathy. What's your name?'
Harry: 'I'm Harry and my sister is Sophie. Sophie's at school.'
Me: 'So is Sophie your big sister?'
Harry: 'Yes. And I got a cat. He's blue.'
Me: 'Is that his name? Blue?'
Harry: 'No! That's his colour. He's blue.'
Me: 'Your cat is blue?'
Harry: 'Yes. My dog is blue.'
Me: 'You've got a blue cat? And a blue dog?'
Harry: 'Yes and me and my mummy and my daddy take him to the park.'
Me: 'Does your sister come too?'
Harry: (thinks for a minute) 'Sometimes'.

This dialogue tells me a lot about Harry and his home environment. He evidently cared a lot about his cat and his dog. Nursery staff confirmed afterwards that his favourite colour is blue and he will colour his pictures blue, ask for the blue cup and play with the blue toys for preference. By designating his animals blue in colour he is demonstrating to me just how important they are in his life. Similarly, even though he started talking about Sophie, his sister, he was less keen to carry on talking about her. Interestingly, when recalling his trips to the park Sophie did not figure as largely as his dog and his mummy and daddy.

There has been growing interest in recent years in how, or if, conditions in the home affect cognitive development. Adoption studies are a good way to evaluate the effects of the home learning environment, as it allows researchers to separate two elements of a child's development – genetics and environment or nature and nurture. For example, Duyme *et al.* (1999), in their studies of child adoption, found that it was the home environment that determined the IQ of the child, rather than the socio-economic status from which they were adopted. It was shown by the EPPE research that the HLE is highly influential on the outcomes for children (Sylva *et al.* 2004) and O'Connor and Scott (2007: 27) went further, stating that improving the parent-child relationship has 'positive effects on the individual and family … and on society as a whole'. Even after leaving the setting and spending time at school, the HLE 'was found to remain a powerful predictor of better cognitive attainment at age 11 even after 6 years in primary school' (Siraj-Blatchford, 2009: 11). This really highlights the enduring effects that the HLE has.

Sylva *et al.* summarise the importance of the HLE as 'what parents do is more important than who parents are' (Sylva *et al.* 2004: 14). This means that it is equally important, if not more important, to encourage SST in the HLE as well as in the setting. For some parents and carers, this will already be occurring naturally. However, in busy homes or with families who have chaotic lifestyles, there may be little or no SST. The research by Hunt *et al.* (2011: 10) found that some parents increased the number of activities they did with their children by 44 per cent once the children had started free childcare places. However, they also discovered that in those families where no parent or carer works full-time, there was a significant decrease in the number of activities that occurred in the HLE. This demonstrates the importance of practitioners having a good relationship with their key families, to ensure that learning opportunities at the setting are continued and supported in the HLE.

Example

Sustained Shared Thinking can be part of the regular routine of a busy home. Because parents and carers are likely to know their children well, they can instigate conversations easily. This can be during regular activities at home such as:

- bath time;
- changing nappies;
- at meal times;
- walking to nursery;
- at bed time.

These are all times when parents and children can spend time together, with the minimum of distractions. Practitioners should support parents and carers in doing this, by explaining the value and importance of the SST and describing the types of interests that could be discussed. For example, bubbles, water and floating could be a good start for conversations at bath time. Practitioners should be careful to explain that SST is not complicated or only to be done by the 'experts'. It is very easy and has great benefits for their child.

Different conversations in the HLE

There are a number of differences between the HLE and an early years' setting that are significant when considering SST. Considered here are some of the advantages and benefits, as well as a brief discussion of the challenges. In general, family members are more likely to understand the context of any conversations because they are with the child most of the time. In addition, there are a number of other advantages of SST in the home learning environment.

Siblings

It is more likely that children will be in 'mixed age groups' at home as they mix with siblings, cousins and the children of family friends. This means that they will have conversations where the more knowledgeable other may well be another, probably older, child. Interestingly, this may mean that the two participants are more attuned than a child and an adult would be, because they have had similar life experiences. Not only will children have more opportunities to practice SST, if parents and carers encourage children to talk together in this way, but this encourages a culture where SST is normal.

Other adults in the home

Children are likely to encounter a whole range of adults in their HLE, from aunts and uncles to grandparents, and even great grandparents. Each of these adults will have different life experiences and knowledge that can be shared with children. Some experiences may be familiar, such as visiting the same places on holiday, whereas others may be totally alien, such as living through a war or living in another country. This will give children a special kind of SST, where the ideas or concepts are very different to their everyday experiences.

Different gender

The vast majority of early years practitioners in the UK are female, which means that children will mainly be talking to women in their setting. However, in the HLE children are more likely to encounter men, whether this is a parent, carer, uncle or granddad, etc. The different perspectives and experiences that men may have will stretch the children's SST experience.

Out and about

During trips out with their parents and carers, children will interact with a number of other adults. This could include adults in the shops, at the park or on the bus. All of these people are likely to have different viewpoints, ways of talking and interacting with children. By experiencing these different conversations, children will learn that not all adults use the same sentence structures, words, etc.

Being the more knowledgeable other

Occasionally children will be the more knowledgeable other in the home. This may be in cases of new technology, where children have less fear of 'getting it wrong' than adults do. Some children seem to have a natural affinity with technology such as iPhones and iPads. In these cases it could well be the child leading the SST, informing and 'educating' the adult.

If there are children of different ages and abilities at home, a child may be a more knowledgeable other to a younger or less able sibling. This gives children the opportunity to direct or inform others during SST, building self-esteem as well as experiencing the process from a different perspective.

THEORY

The research entitled 'Provider influence on the early home learning environment (EHLE)' commissioned by the Department for Children, Schools and Families, aimed to identify the most effective strategies in supporting parents in the early home learning environment. Summarised here are some of their findings (Hunt *et al.* 2011: 50 onwards) with some commentary on how practitioners in settings can do this in practice.

One of the questions asked of parents was: 'What do you want from staff at the setting that your child attends?'

- Provide more information. This could be information about activities that can be done at home, such as recipes for play dough or ideas for rainy days. For most settings this would only need minimal extra work, such as simply photocopying the planning sheet or play dough recipe and having it available to pick up in the signing-in area. Practitioners could point parents towards activities that their child has particularly enjoyed.

- Give more feedback. This was both for concerns but also a brief 'progress review' of how their child has done during the day. Practitioners can explain the type of SST that has happened during the day and also provide ideas on how to extend this at home. For example: 'we were talking about putting things in envelopes today and the post box. Could you show James where the post box is on the way home, please? He could have a look to see where the letters go'.

- Help with behaviour and socialisation. Many parents look to practitioners as the experts when it comes to challenging behaviour and strategies for dealing with this. Practitioners can explain how to use SST to resolve conflict and work out differences. Practitioners may not be aware of how much of a positive difference this can make to parents' and carers' home life.

- Communicate more. It is easier than ever to communicate with parents and carers. Text messages sent in bulk via the computer (for when snow shuts the setting for example), website notices, photos and video clips sent (securely) to mobile phones and emails. This could be information leaflets about SST or evening events.

Then parents and carers were asked: 'What have practitioners done that has changed what you do at home with your child to help them to learn?'

- Given information and resources. This is highly valued by parents and carers and is relatively simple. As well as practical activities, practitioners can give information on the value of SST or schematic play.

- Ideas for learning activities. The value of SST can be emphasised through-out all activities, for both the child and the adult. The adult may learn how the child understands the world and this also supports self-esteem.

Challenges in the HLE

Practitioners who are skilled at SST will give the child their full attention, be led by the child's interest and will be finding ways of extending knowl-edge between them. However, this may not be the case in the home learning environment.

Homes can be very busy places, with siblings, other family members, jobs to do and places to go to. It is not always possible to find a quiet, distraction-free place to talk, especially if this is in competition with the TV, DVDs or video games. After a day at nursery or with the childminder, children may not feel like talking, but would prefer to have some quiet time to themselves. This can be frustrating for parents and carers, who may want to talk about how the child's day has been, what they have done and who they have played with. However, it is very important for children to have quiet time when they can assimilate and understand their experiences from the day. It can be difficult to appreciate this and parents and carers may be put off trying to initiate conversations if their child does not show any interest.

Conversely, it could be that when children get home they are so busy doing other things (having friends to visit, going out, shopping, etc.) that parents don't feel they have time to 'just' talk to their child. It could be advantageous to explain the benefits of SST to parents and carers, so they are aware that it is time well spent and try to make time for it when they get home.

Cultural norms

Practitioners should be careful not to superimpose their own 'cultural norms' onto the child's family. They should be aware that the child's experiences at home might be very different to those at their setting. For example, there are cultures where interacting with adults and giving eye contact would be con-sidered disrespectful, or where boys finish eating before girls are allowed to eat (Zussman 2012). It can be confusing for a child to be presented at nursery with something very different to their home customs, particularly if there have been no explanations. It is always better to work with the family, so there are no misunderstandings.

Similarly, it can be confusing for families if the practitioners are asking them to do something different. Traditionally, in most cultures, child rearing is female work. Even in the UK, 87 per cent of dads still don't read to their children (Douglas 2013). Therefore, if practitioners ask dads to take on some activities at home, this may be met with confusion. Tekin (2011) found that there was little research on parental involvement in Turkey. However, the result of his own research demonstrated that parents believed they 'should be highly active in their young children's education' (Tekin 2011: 1324). Furthermore, the results showed that parents believed that they would be good at it and this would make a positive difference. These results echo the types of beliefs that would be found with Western counterparts, but practitioners should not assume that they understand the culture and should check first.

THEORY

Another culture that practitioners may come across is Deaf (with a capital D) culture. This is a thriving community in the UK that values the culture and identity of Deaf peoples and share a sense of belonging. The British Deaf Association (BDA) has been supporting the community since 1890, with their stated cornerstones being: the language, community, identity and heritage of Deaf people.

The BDA's vision is: 'Deaf people fully participating and contributing as equal and valued citizens in the wider society' and they aim to achieve this through:

- improving the quality of life by empowering Deaf individuals and groups;
- enhancing freedom, equality and diversity;
- protecting and promoting BSL.

To find out more about Deaf culture visit: http://www.bda.org.uk/About_Us/BDA_-_Our_Values

---

Books and artefacts from other cultures can start conversations that may lead to SST, as well as making children feel respected and part of the setting community. Lindon (2005: 1) advises sourcing books that include images from other cultures, but to be aware that children may 'feel excluded' if 'people like me' only appear in books about 'children from other lands'.

English as an Additional Language (EAL)

Children who have English as an Additional Language will not all be alike. Some may have no spoken English, but with good understanding, whereas others may have very good English but their home language is different. Practitioners should be aware that bilingualism, or even multilingualism, is an asset for the child (DCSF 2007), and should be supported wherever possible. Practitioners should be aware of the level of home language from the time that a child starts at the setting (in case there is a global speech and language developmental problem) as well as their progress in English. Just as practitioners should 'tune into' the child's interests, they should also 'tune into the family'. This is a vital way of supporting the child in all aspects of learning and development. Siraj-Blatchford (2007: 3) argues that the social theories of early childhood education are becoming more influential, over the more traditional Piagetian views that have held such sway previously. As a result of this, she suggests that 'It isn't actually necessary to accept the dominant role that language may take in the learning processes' and that children will still learn through social contexts. This is an important view to note. Practitioners who are not confident with trying SST with a child who has EAL should note that the verbal language is not absolutely vital in order to learn about PSED, for example. The importance of SST is not to check or test their use of spoken English, but to share concepts and ideas and this can be done non-verbally, using gestures and objects.

The home language of a child is an essential link to their family, culture and traditions. It is important to support and develop their home language (DfE 2012) to ensure these lines of communication with families are still being used, so parents can share thoughts and ideas with their children to help 'shape, guide and influence their lives' (DCSF 2007: 4). The role of SST is not to replace the home language with English, but to explore ideas and concepts.

Example

English as an Additional Language – practical ideas

Children always understand any language before they can speak it. Therefore, it is important that practitioners still talk to children who have EAL so they can hear the rhythm of the language and the vocabulary. Although this may not strictly be SST, it is a way of modelling sustained dialogues to children. 'Children need to hear language used in a meaningful context before they can rehearse and use it themselves' (DCSF 2007: 15).

Make sure that names are correctly pronounced (DCSF 2007: 8) and that the correct form or name is being used. It could be that the name that parents and carers use is a private name that should only be used by family. This can be detailed on the registration form, but it is polite for practitioners to check this with the family verbally as well. Pronunciation is very important as incorrectly pronounced words may change their meaning.

Think about the location of the SST. Many children are happier talking outside, where there is less pressure to 'perform', than they are at circle time, for instance. Sustained Shared Thinking may happen more naturally in the home corner (especially if it reflects the child's culture), when the child is in control of the play.

Two very useful techniques that practitioners can use to develop SST are 'self-talk' and 'parallel talk' (Bayley and Broadbent 2013). Self-talk is talking to yourself as you plan, having a running commentary on what is happening or verbalisation of the action that you are seeing. Once a child is comfortable with this, then the practitioner can move on to parallel talk, where the practitioner gives a commentary on the child's play. Note that this should not be judgmental, but should be enthusiastic and supportive. These techniques mirror one half of the SST, so when your child is confident enough to talk, they will have already experienced the process.

Most importantly, allow your child time to absorb the language around them, not rushing him or her into SST. But be ready to respond as soon as he or she initiates a conversation.

Practitioners should make sure that they have active two-way conversations with the parents, carers and extended family of the children in their care. It would be very easy to assume that they know what the families want – and get it wrong! For example, it could be assumed that parents would want you to learn their home language to use in the setting. However, some parents may send their children to a predominantly English-speaking setting so their child can hear the language and learn from it. Similarly, it would be easy to assume that the family celebrates all the religious festivals of their faith, but it could be they only celebrate the major festivals and not the minor ones.

Culture and EAL are two areas where children are likely to be more knowledgeable than the practitioners. Therefore, there could be times during the SST when the flow of information is from the child to the practitioner.

Conclusions

The home learning environment (HLE) will be as diverse as the children who attend the setting. Practitioners should not make assumptions about the HLE and the sorts of experiences that children may be having. As Siraj-Blatchford notes (2009: 12) 'there are many disadvantaged children in even the wealthiest of countries that deserve our very best pedagogical efforts when they attend pre-school settings'.

There are many advantages for children's learning and development in the HLE, including sharing conversations with a wider range of adults and children of other ages. It could well be that the child is the more knowledgeable other in these circumstances, and may instigate or lead the SST. This is valuable experience, as well as being good for self-esteem and self-confidence. The HLE is one of the areas where the child is the expert who understands the cultural norms, language and traditions of the environment. Practitioners should respect this and can use it during their SST to encourage the child to lead the two-way dialogue.

Further reading

Hartas, D. (2012) 'Inequality and the home learning environment: predictions about seven-year-olds' language and literacy'. *British Educational Research Journal* Vol. 38, Iss. 5 pp. 859–879.

Frumkin, L. (2013) 'Young children's cognitive achievement: home learning environment, language and ethnic background'. *Journal of Early Childhood Research* Vol. 11, No. 3 pp. 222–235.

9 Concluding thoughts

During learning a human being is an active thinker, and not a passive recipient, and, in the same vein, it could be argued that developing thinking is about developing capabilities for learning.

(Bernhard 2007: 1)

Introduction

This chapter evaluates SST and highlights the benefits, whatever sort of setting you have and wherever you work with young children. These are linked to the personal, social and emotional development of the child.

Sustained Shared Thinking and the curriculum

Sustained Shared Thinking throughout this book has been closely linked to the English curriculum for the Early Years Foundation Stage (EYFS). However, it is equally applicable to other curricula because it is based on the longitudinal research of the EPPE project. The EPPE project followed 3,000 children through their early years settings and then throughout their primary education. At the time (2004) it was the largest research project in Europe.

The EYFS identifies personal, social and emotional development (PSED) and communication and language as two Prime Areas because they are 'crucial for igniting children's curiosity and enthusiasm for learning, and for building their capacity to learn, form relationships and thrive' (DfE 2012). These are the central building blocks for any child's learning and development.

Benefits of SST

The benefits of SST have been discussed throughout the book. Here is a recap and review of some of the benefits and why you should be using SST every day in your setting.

Ease of use

Sustained Shared Thinking is free; you do not need to buy any special equipment. All you need are practitioners who are interested in interacting with children and children who enjoy being listened to. Practitioners may benefit from training on active listening and advice on when to intervene in children's play. However, on the whole, is it a skill that is best learnt through practice.

The vast majority of practitioners naturally enjoy being with children and enjoy seeing them learn and develop, so there is an intrinsic motivation for practitioners to improve their SST skills.

Sustained Shared Thinking is suitable for children and babies of all ages. It is a skill that can be used from the baby room to Reception and with the full range of children in a child-minder's or nanny's care. Practitioners may need to consider how their skills need to be adapted for each age range, but this will happen whenever you move rooms or welcome a child of a different age to your setting.

Talking to, and listening to, a young child is an enjoyable experience. It is fascinating to observe how children perceive the world and make sense of all the experiences that they have. It can make you think about things you take for granted (spring will follow winter, caterpillars turning into butterflies) and it can sometimes give you new enjoyment in the seemingly mundane (for example, the beautiful colours of autumn leaves).

Improving children's personal, social and emotional development

As adults we know that we learn best when relaxed, eager to learn and with companionable people. This is even more true for children, because they still need to practice strategies for coping with situations where they are not comfortable.

Sustained Shared Thinking builds self-esteem by valuing children's thoughts and views with active listening and in a respectful way. Children know that practitioners have time to spend listening to them and responding positively. Self-confidence is built through practising SST with a range of adults and children, both within the setting and in the home learning environment. Similarly, a mastery disposition is fostered through being listened to, being allowed to investigate different ways to solve a problem and examining different concepts – in a safe and respectful environment. Children know that practitioners are not looking for the 'right' answer with SST, but are genuinely working through a problem together.

If SST is used for conflict resolution and negotiation, these are excellent social skills that can be used throughout life. Resilience, or the ability to 'bounce back' from situations, has been shown to originate in a child's early years (Goleman 1998). Sustained Shared Thinking can cultivate this by allowing children to talk through problems, realise there may be many solutions and having the support of respectful practitioners.

Understanding the child

From a practitioner's point of view, SST is vital in getting to know children and in tuning in to their ideas and interests. There will be times when the child is the more knowledgeable other such as, for example, in cultural aspects and the home learning environment. Practitioners can learn from this, informing them of the child's motivation to learn. For example, cuing in to a child's fascination with mini-beasts can lead onto number work, language development, discussion about habitats, etc.

More effective planning

Planning the environment, continuous provision, activities and resources is much easier when you know what the children enjoy doing – and why they enjoy doing it. Sustained Shared Thinking can give you these answers, and older children can co-construct planning through using SST with the practitioners.

Reflective practice

Sustained Shared Thinking supports a practitioner's reflective practice. When you are sharing thoughts with children and extending their thinking, you will be reflecting on your own knowledge and life experiences. In addition, if you share the SST with a critical friend, you can reflect on how to improve your interactions and your practice.

▋ Some personal reflections

I distinctly remember the first time I became aware of SST as a process or approach to working with children. I had been working at nursery for a number of years, and had volunteered at the school Reception class in the years before that, so I had been working with young children for some time. It was now time to move on to the next level and get my Early Years Professional Status. This was 2007, so the Status was in its infancy and there was very little written guidance, articles or books on the subject. I had to evidence 'Sustained Shared Thinking' (Standard 16 – some things never leave you!).

I happened to be thinking about this as I answered the door to Liam and his Granddad. Liam very proudly showed me an enormous conker he had picked up on the way to nursery.

'Look, conker.'

'Wow,' I replied, 'that really is the biggest conker!'

'Big tree,' stated Liam.

'They do come from big trees, don't they? Do you know what the tree is called?'

And Liam gave me a strange look, a bit puzzled and a bit disappointed.

'It's a horse chestnut tree,' I informed him.

By now Liam was looking distinctly miffed – and I knew then that something had gone wrong.

Liam's Granddad leaned into the conversation and explained how they had walked to nursery the long way round, past the big tree, and how excited Liam had been to discover that a different path could still end up at nursery. His conker was just a way of showing me that he had been past the Big Tree.

It dawned on me at that point that I hadn't practiced Sustained Shared Thinking – just the opposite – I had imposed my assumptions and views on Liam, without listening or sharing ideas at all. Although I did return to Liam at a later time and asked all about his walk to nursery, the moment had gone and it made me realise how fleeting and precious these moments could be.

On reflecting afterwards, and even though I had a number of years' experience across a range of ages and settings, I had still not appreciated the subtlety and strength of SST until I had started studying for my EYPS. As I became more adept at spotting opportunities for SST, I found that they were everywhere.

Connor was playing on the slide outside, and he noticed that his hair was standing up when he got to the bottom of the slide. Having mentioned this, we investigated rubbing the slide with material and seeing what happened. He was fascinated by the static all afternoon and went down the slide multiple times to keep testing his theory. We talked about this, watched other children and touched fingers to see what the static felt like at the end of the slide.

After we had come indoors I had forgotten about this, and Connor had gone to onto to play with other things. It wasn't mentioned for the rest of the day.

However, the next day, the first thing Connor wanted to do was to go outdoors with me to 'test the slide'. This was without any prompting or reminders. It was obvious that he had been thinking about his experiences since the previous day and he wanted to carry on our testing. To have his thinking carry over to the next day was truly sustained!

Jacob and his family had been away for a long weekend, and when he came back into nursery he was full of his adventures. He had been talking about taking a boat into the water on a lake (or river, he couldn't decide which) and how the flag on the boat looked different to normal.

I had assumed that the family had been to North Wales, where there is a dragon on the flag and boats. However, as we talked more about his adventures and the details of his weekend it became obvious that my assumptions were wrong. Jacob stated that the flag was blue and he was quite definite about this, so it couldn't be the green, red and white Welsh flag. He told me all about the large trees that smelled like an air freshener, that were on the water's edge, so that probably ruled out the seaside.

After drawing both the flag and a picture of the boat I began to realise that he had probably been to another country, possibly Sweden. I finally thought to ask if he'd been on a plane, which he confirmed that he had (although this was less important to him than the boat). When his mum came to pick him up that evening, she explained that they had relatives in Sweden and had visited their summer house, where they kept a boat on a lake.

Without the SST to solve the riddle of the flag and the location of the boat, I would still be under the assumption that Jacob had visited North Wales and not Sweden. However, once this had been established, we were able to go on to investigate different flags, the way that boats look and the location of different places around the globe. Jacob took this into map making and spent many weeks after that creating maps or drawings of places he had visited.

Of course, these are exceptional examples, and the majority of SST occurs in the every-day occurrences of nursery or setting life. For example, talking while sitting at an activity, chatting at snack time and playing outdoors.

What to do next

The best way to implement SST is to build it into your daily practice and to be always looking out for opportunities to talk to and actively listen to your children. However, this can often be a challenge during the busy day with your children and reinforcing techniques like SST can often get forgotten. So, one of the best ways of ensuring this happens is to use your reflective practice. At the end of each day, reflect back on your interactions with your children.

- Did you have some successful SST?
- Why was it successful and how could you repeat that next time?

- Were there other opportunities for SST that you could capitalise on next time?
- How could you have extended a child's thought processes?

Ask your critical friend to review these with you.

From these reflections you will be able to see where your strengths are (you may be particularly good at SST during lunch time with the children) and the areas for development.

Once you have identified areas for development, watch to see if there is another practitioner in the setting, or in your network, who is good in this area. Ask to peer observe them and learn how they do this. For example, if you find it hard to find opportunities for SST in mathematical areas, find a colleague who is confident in this area and is willing to be observed doing this.

If you are working with older children, ask them how your SST was today. Did you spend time listening and talking with them? When did you problem solve and extend concepts? Did the children enjoy it and what would they like more of?

Conclusions

You can find opportunities to engage children with SST, whatever their age, ability, indoors, outdoors, in a large busy nursery or the quiet of a child-minder's front room. Sustained Shared Thinking helps to co-construct children's thoughts and is respectful of both participants. It is important for children's learning and development. The huge benefits for such an enjoyable activity are amazing.

References

Ainsworth, M. and Bell, S. (1970) 'Attachment, Exploration, and Separation: Illustrated by the Behavior of One-year-olds in a Strange Situation'. *Child Development*, Vol. 41, Iss. 1, pp. 49–67.

Allen, P. (2012) (2nd Ed. updated by Debbie Chalmers) *Science and Technology for the Early Years: Purposeful Play Activities*. Dunstable: Brilliant Books.

Bayley, R. and Broadbent, L. (2013) 'Child Initiated Learning and Developing Children's Talk' in Featherstone, S. (2013) *Like Bees, not Butterflies*. London: Bloomsbury.

Beeley, K. (2009) *Using Empathy Dolls*. London: A&C Black Publishing.

Belton, T. (2008) 'A Fresh Look at Boredom'. *Primary Leadership Today*, Issue 13.

Bernhard, J. (2007) *Thinking and Learning through Technology: Mediating Tools in Science and Engineering Education*. Conference paper from The 13th International Conference on Thinking Norrköping, Sweden June 17–21, 2007. Available from http://www.ep.liu.se/ecp_article/index.en.aspx?issue=021; vol=2;article=003 (last accessed 8 January 2014).

Bilton, H. (2004) *Playing Outside. Activities, Ideas and Inspiration for the Early Years*. London: David Fulton Publishers.

Bowlby, J. (1969) *Attachment and Loss*. New York: Basic Books.

Bronfenbrenner, U. (1979) *The Ecology of Human Development: Experiments by Nature and Design*. Harvard: Harvard University Press.

Bruce, T. (2004) *Cultivating Creativity*. London: Hodder Education.

Bruce, T. (2005) 'Ten Principles of the Pioneers: The Bedrock of the Early Childhood Traditions' in Bruce, T. *Early Childhood Education* (pp. 11–33). London: Hodder Arnold.

Bruner, J. (1983) *Child's Talk: Learning to use Language*. New York: Norton.

Bruner, J. (1986) *Actual Minds, Possible Worlds*. Harvard: Harvard University Press.

BSL (2013) *What is British Sign Language?* Available from: http://www.british-sign.co.uk/bsl-british-sign-language/what-is-british-sign-language (last accessed on 22 October 2013).

Bupa's Health Information Team (2011) *Glue Ear*. Available from: http://www.bupa.co.uk/individuals/health-information/directory/g/otitis-media (last accessed on 31 May 2013).

Chilvers, D. (2012) *Playing to Learn: A Guide to Child-led Play and its Importance for Thinking and Learning*. London: ATL.

Chomsky, N. (1965) *Aspects of the Theory of Syntax*. Cambridge, MA: MIT Press.

Clare, A. (2012) *Creating a Learning Environment for Babies and Toddlers*. London: Sage.

Clark, A. (2001) *The Project Approach: Three Avenues of Engagement*. Available from: http://ecap.crc.illinois.edu/pubs/katzsym/annmarie.pdf (last accessed on 22 October 2013).

Clarke, J. (2007) *Sustaining Shared Thinking*. London: Featherstone Publishing.

Claxton, G. and Carr, M. (2004) 'A Framework for Teaching Learning: the Dynamics of Disposition'. *Early Years* Vol. 24, Iss. 1, pp. 87–97.

Claxton, G. (2007) 'Expanding Young People's Capacity to Learn'. *British Journal of Educational Studies* Vol. 55, No. 2, pp. 1–20.

Coates, G. (2009) *Notes on Communication: a few Thoughts about the Way we Interact with the People we Meet*. Free ebook available from www.wanterfall.com.

Constable, K. and Green, S. (2013) *Planning for Schematic Learning in the Early Years: A Practical Guide*. London: Routledge.

Cooper, L. and Doherty, J. (2010) *Physical Development (Supporting Development in the Early Years Foundation Stage)*. London: Continuum.

Csikszentmihalyi, M. (2002) *Flow*. London: Rider Books.

Curtiss, S. (1977) *Genie: A Psycholinguistic Study of a Modern-Day "Wild Child"*. New York: Academic Press.

David, T., Goouch, K., Powell, S. and Abbott, L. (2003) *Birth to Three Matters: A Review of the Literature compiled to inform The Framework to Support Children in their Earliest Years*. Nottingham: DfES Publications.

Department for Children, Education, Lifelong Learning and Skills (2008) *Welsh Language Development*. Cardiff: Welsh Assembly Government.

Department for Children, Families and Schools (2008) *Social and Emotional Aspects of Development*. Nottingham: DCSF Publications.

DCSF (2007) *Supporting Children Learning English as an Additional Language Guidance for Practitioners in the Early Years Foundation Stage*. Nottingham: DCSF Publications.

DCSF Publications (2008a) *Child Development Overview*. Nottingham: DCSF.

DCSF Publications (2008b) *Social and Emotional Aspects of Development (SEAD) Guidance for Practitioners Working in the Foundation Stage*. Nottingham: DCSF.

DCSF Publications (2008c) *Principles into Practice Cards*. Nottingham: DCSF.

Department for Education (2012) *Statutory Framework for the Early Years Foundation Stage* available online only from: http://media.education.gov.uk/assets/files/pdf/eyfs%20statutory%20framework%20march%202012.pdf (last accessed 8 January 2014).

Department for Education (2013) *National Curriculum Assessments: Early Years Foundation Stage Profile Handbook 2014*. Available from: http://www.education.gov.uk/schools/teachingandlearning/assessment (last accessed 22 October 2013).

Dinneen, F. (2009) 'Does Relationship Training for Caregivers Enhance Young Children's Learning and Language?' in Papatheodorou, T. and Moyles, J. *Learning Together in the Early Years: Exploring Relational Pedagogy*. London: Routledge.

Doherty, J. and Bailey, R. (2002) *Supporting Physical Development and Physical Education in the Early Years*. Maidenhead: Open University.

Douglas, I. (2013) *Fathers Cut Themselves off by Not Reading to their Children*. The *Daily Telegraph* 25 February 2013. Available online from: http://www.telegraph.co.uk/men/relationships/fatherhood/9888637/Fathers-cut-themselves-off-by-not-reading-to-their-children.html (last accessed on 16 October 2013).

Dowling, M. (2010) *Young Children's Personal, Social and Emotional Development* (3rd Ed.). London: Sage.

Dowling, M. (2013) *Young Children's Thinking*. London: Sage.

Dubiel, J. (2012) 'Learning & Development: How Children Learn'. *Nursery World*, 2–15 April, 2012, pp. 19–23.

Duyme, M., Dumaret, A.C. and Tomkiewicz, T.C. (1999) 'How Can we Boost IQs of "Dull Children"? A Late Adoption Study'. *Proceedings of the National Academy of Sciences*, Vol. 96, pp. 8790–4.

Early Education (2012) *Development Matters in the Early Years Foundation Stage* (EYFS). London: Early Education.

Edmond, N. and Price, M. (Eds) (2012) *Integrated Working with Children and Young People: Supporting Development from Birth to Nineteen*. London: Sage.

Einarsdottir, J., Dockett, S. and Perry, B. (2009) 'Making Meaning: Children's Perspectives Expressed through Drawings'. *Early Child Development and Care*, Vol. 179, Iss. 2, pp. 217–232.

ELCE (2013) *What is Makaton?* Available from: http://www.elce.org/index.php?option=com_content&view=article&id=68&Itemid=103 (last accessed on 22 October 2013).

Fleming, S., Dolan, R. and Frith, C. (2012) 'Metacognition: Computation, Biology and Function'. *Philosophical Transactions of the Royal Society* Vol. 367, pp. 1280–1286.

Flewitt, R. (2013) *Early Literacy: A Broader Vision*. Available from TACTYC: http://eprints.ncrm.ac.uk/3132/1/flewitt_occasional%2Dpaper3.pdf (last accessed on 26 October 2013).

Fox, N. (2011) *Lipreading For Children: Challenges and Benefits*. Available from: http://www.irishdeafkids.ie/2011/lipreading-for-children (last accessed 10 July 2013).

Frazier, B., Gelman, S. and Wellman, H. (2009) 'Pre-schoolers' Search for Explanatory Information within Adult-child Conversation'. *Child Development* Vol. 80, Iss. 6, pp. 1592–1611.

Freeman, K. and Hartshorne, M. (2009) *Speech, Language and Communication Needs and the Early Years*. Available from iCan: http://www.ican.org.uk (last accessed 11 July 2013).

Fumoto, H., Robson, S., Greenfield, S. and Hargreaves, D. (2012) *Young Children's Creative Thinking*. London: Sage.

Gardner, H. (1983) *Frames of Mind: The Theory of Multiple Intelligences*. New York: Basic Books.

Gardner, H., Kornhaber, M. and Wake, W. (1996) *Intelligence. Multiple Perspectives*. Fort Worth: Harcourt Brace.

Gerhardt, S. (2004) *Why Love Matters*. London: Routledge.

Gifford, S. (2004) 'A New Mathematics Pedagogy for the Early Years: in Search of Principles for Practice'. *International Journal of Early Years Education* Vol. 12, No. 2, pp. 99–115.

Glazzard, J., Chadwick, D., Webster, A. and Percival, J. (2010) *Assessment for Learning in the Early Years Foundation Stage*. London: Sage.

Goldman, A. (2012) 'Theory of Mind' in Margolis, E., Samuels, R. and Stich, S. *Oxford Handbook of Philosophy and Cognitive Science*. Oxford: Oxford University Press.

Goleman, D. (1998) *Working with Emotional Intelligence*. New York: Bantam Dell.

Goleman, D. (2006) *Social Intelligence. The New Science of Human Relationships* London: Random House.

Gopnik, A. (2009) 'Your Baby Is Smarter Than You Think' *The New York Times* (16 August 2009). Available from: http://www.nytimes.com/2009/08/16/opinion/16gopnik.html?pagewanted=print (last accessed on 21 June 2013).

Gopnik, A. (2011) *What Do Babies Think?* Available from: http://www.ted.com/talks/alison_gopnik_what_do_babies_think.html (last accessed on 10 July 2013).

Greenland, P. (2009) *Jabadao: Developmental Movement Play*. Leeds: Jabadao.

Greenland, P. (2013) 'Physical Development' in Veale, F. (Ed.) *Early Years for Levels 4&5*. Maidenhead: Hodder Education.

Hall, J. (2005) *Neuroscience and Education. A Review of the Contribution of Brain Science to Teaching and Learning: SCRE Research Report No 121*. Glasgow: Glasgow University.

Hargie, O. (2011) *Skilled Interpersonal Communication* (5th Ed.). London: Routledge.

HighScope (2013) *How We Teach*. Available from: http://www.highscope. org/Content.asp?ContentId=171 (last accessed on 9 July 2013).

Hunt, S., Virgo, S., Klett-Davies, M., Page, A., and Apps, J. (2011) *Provider Influence on the Early Home Learning Environment (EHLE)* DFE-RBX-10-11. London: DFE Publications.

Isbell, R. and Raine, S. (2012) *Creativity and the Arts with Young Children* (3rd Ed.) Belmont: Wadsworth Publishing Co Inc.

Jarman, E. (2009) *A Place to Talk Outside*. London: A&C Black.

Jarman, E. (2012) *Creating Optimum Conditions for Learning*. Available from: http://www.elizabethjarmantraining.co.uk/index.php?option=com_cont ent&view=article&id=2&Itemid=6 (last accessed on 24 October 2013).

Johnson, M. and Jones, M. (2012) *Supporting Quiet Children: Exciting Ideas and Activities to Help 'Reluctant Talkers' Become 'Confident Talkers'*. Birmingham: Laurence Educational Publications.

Jones, D. (2007) 'Speaking, Listening, Planning and Assessing: the Teacher's Role in Developing Metacognitive Awareness'. *Early Child Development and Care* Vol. 177, Iss. 6, pp. 569–579.

Jones, M. (2013) *Using Small Talk, Chat, Conversation and Discussion to Help Children and Adults become Better Communicators: With a Helping Hand from D.H. Lawrence and Britta and Shirley from Community*. Available from: http://www. talk4meaning.co.uk/2013/07/using-small-talk-chat-conversation-and-discussion-to-help-children-and-adults-become-better-communicators-with-a-helping-hand-from-d-h-lawrence-and-britta-and-shirley-from-community (last accessed on 12 July 2013).

Kanira, E. and Ward, K. (2013) 'Behaviour and Behaviour Management in Early Years' in Veale, F. (Ed.) *Early Years for Levels 4 & 5 and the Foundation Degree*. Abingdon: Hodder Education.

Katz, L. and Chard, S. (2000) *Engaging Children's Minds* (2nd Ed.). Connecticut: Ablex Publishing Corporation.

Klein, M. (1932) *The Psycho-analysis of Children*. London: Hogarth Press.

Kulick, D. (1992) *Language Shift and Cultural Reproduction: Socialization, Self, and Syncretism in a Papua New Guinean Village*. New York: Cambridge University Press.

Laevers, F. (1994) *The Leuven Involvement Scale for Young Children LIS-YC Manual Experiential Education Series, No. 1*. Belgium: Centre for Experiential Education, Leuven.

Laevers, F. (2005a) *Deep-level-learning and the Experiential Approach in Early Childhood and Primary Education*. Belgium: Katholieke Universiteit Research Centre for Early Childhood and Primary Education, Leuven.

Laevers, F. (Ed.) (2005b) *Wellbeing and Involvement in Care Settings. A Process-oriented Self-evaluation Instrument*. Belgium: Research Centre for Experiential Education, Leuven University.

Laevers, F. (2011) 'Experiential Education: Making Care and Education More Effective through Well-being and Involvement', Bennett, J. topic Ed. in: Tremblay, R.E., Boivin, M., Peters, R.Dev. and Barr, R.G. Eds *Encyclopedia on Early Childhood Development* [online]. Montreal, Quebec: Centre of Excellence for Early Childhood Development and Strategic Knowledge Cluster on Early Child Development; 2011: 1–5. Available at: http://www.child-encyclopedia.com/documents/LaeversANGxp1.pdf (last accessed 13 January 2014).

Levine, J. (2011) 'Finnishing School – How an Anti-Tiger Mother Approach to Education Helps Finland turn out a Better-than-average Workforce', *Time Magazine* [online]. Available from: http://content.time.com/time/magazine/article/0,9171,2062465,00.html (last accessed on 16 June 2013).

Lindon, J. (2005) *Cultural Diversity in the Early Years*. Available from: http://www.communityplaythings.co.uk/learning-library/articles/cultural-diversity-in-the-early-years (last accessed on 22 September 2013).

Lindon, J. (2012a) *What Does it Mean to be Two?* (revised Ed.). London: MA Publishing.

Lindon, J. (2012b) *Reflective Practice and Early Years Professionalism: Linking Theory and Practice*. London: Hodder Education.

Lubell, K.M., Lofton, T. and Singer, H.H. (2008) *Promoting Healthy Parenting Practices Across Cultural Groups: A CDC Research Brief*. Atlanta (GA): Centers for Disease Control and Prevention, National Center for Injury Prevention and Control.

Main, M. and Solomon, J. (1986) 'Discovery of an Insecure-disorganized/Disoriented Pattern' in: Brazelton, T. and Yogman, M. (Eds.) *Affective Development in Infancy*. Norwood, NJ: Ablex Publishing Corporation.

Mercer, N. and Sams, C. (2006) 'Teaching Children How to Use Language to Solve Maths Problems'. *Language and Education* Vol. 20, No. 6, pp. 507–528.

Mix, K., Moore, J. and Holcomb, E. (2011) 'One-to-One Play Promotes Numerical Equivalence Concepts'. *Journal of Cognition and Development*, Vol. 12, No. 4, pp. 463–480.

Moss, P. and Petrie, P. (2006) *From Children's Spaces to Children's Services*. London: Routledge Falmer.

Moyles, J. (2010) *The Excellence of Play*. Maidenhead: Open University Press.

Nucci, L. (2008) *Moral Development and Moral Education: An Overview*. Available from: http://tigger.uic.edu/~lnucci/MoralEd/overview.html (last accessed on 10 July 2013).

Nutbrown, C. and Hannon, P. (2011) *The Aims, Structure and Framework of the Sheffield REAL Project*. Available at: www.real-online.group.shef.ac.uk (last accessed on 4 August 2013).

Nutkins, S., McDonald, C. and Stephen, M. (2013) *Early Childhood Education and Care: An Introduction*. London: Sage.

Oates, J., Karmiloff-Smith, A. and Johnson, M. (2012) *Developing Brains*. Milton Keynes: The Open University.

O'Connor, T. and Scott, S. (2007) *Parenting and Outcomes for Children*. New York: The Joseph Rowntree Foundation.

Panter-Brick, C. and Leckman, J. (2013) 'Editorial Commentary: Resilience in Child Development – Interconnected Pathways to Wellbeing'. *Journal of Child Psychology and Psychiatry* 54: 4, pp. 333–336.

Papatheodorou T. and Moyles, J. (2009) *Learning Together in the Early Years*. London: Routledge.

Parents Early Education Partnership (PEEP) (2013) *Learning Together – From the Start*. Available from: http://www.peep.org.uk/temp/PEEPspOverview.pdf (last accessed on 4 August 2013).

Park, E. and King, K. (2003) ERIC DIGEST *Cultural Diversity and Language Socialization in the Early Years*. Available at http://www.cal.org/resources/digest/digest_pdfs/0313park.pdf (last accessed on 20 June 2013).

Percival, J. (2010) 'Personalised Learning: Looking at Children Holistically' in Glazzard, J., Chadwick, D., Webster, A. and Percival, J. (2010) *Assessment for Learning in the Early Years Foundation Stage*. London: Sage.

Perry, B. and Szalavitz, M. (2006) *The Boy who was Raised as a Dog*. New York: Basic Books.

Petrie, P., Boddy, J., Cameron, C., Wigfall, V., Simon, A. (2006) *Working with Children in Care: European Perspectives*. Maidenhead: Open University Press.

Piaget, J. and Inhelder, B. (1969) *Psychology of the Child*. New York: Basic Books.

Piaget, J. (1965) *Moral Judgement of the Child*. New York: Free Press.

Richardson, H. (2013) *Children Should be Allowed to get Bored, Expert Says*. Available online: http://www.bbc.co.uk/news/education-21895704 (last accessed on 13 October 2013).

Roberts, R. D., Zeidner, M. and Matthews, G. (2001) 'Does Emotional Intelligence Meet Traditional Standards for an Intelligence? Some New Data and Conclusions'. *Emotion*, Vol. 1, No. 3, pp. 196–231.

Roberts, R. (2010) *Wellbeing from Birth*. London: Sage.

Robinson, K. (2009) *The Element*. London: Penguin.

Robinson, K. (2013) *How to Escape Education's Death Valley.* Available at: http://www.ted.com/talks/ken_robinson_how_to_escape_education_s_death_valley.html?quote=2162 (last accessed on 22 September 2013).

Robson, S. (2006) *Developing Thinking and Understanding in Young Children.* London: Routledge.

Robson, S. (2012) *Developing Thinking and Understanding in Young Children: An Introduction for Students.* London: Routledge.

Robson, S. and Rowe, V. (2012) 'Observing Young Children's Creative Thinking: Engagement, Involvement and Persistence'. *International Journal of Early Years Education*, Vol. 20, Iss. 4, pp. 349–364.

Rose, J. and Rogers, S. (2012) *The Role of the Adult in Early Years Settings.* Maidenhead: Open University Press.

Rymer, R. (1993) *Genie: An Abused Child's Flight from Silence.* New York: Harper-Collins Publishers.

Rymer, R. (1994) *Genie: A Scientific Tragedy.* New York: First HarperPerennial.

Salmon, A. and Lucas, T. (2011) 'Exploring Young Children's Conceptions about Thinking'. *Journal of Research in Childhood Education* Vol. 25, Iss. 4, pp. 364–375.

Sargent, M. (2011a) *Using Projects to Promote Sustained Shared Thinking.* London: Practical Pre-school Books.

Sargent, M. (2011b) *Assessment for Learning in the EYFS.* London: Featherstone Education.

Stewart, N. (2011) *How Children Learn. The Characteristics of Effective Learning.* London: Early Education.

Schaffer, R. (1996) 'Joint Involvement Episodes as Context for Development' in Daniels, H. *An Introduction to Vygotsky.* London: Routledge.

Schon, D. (1983) *The Reflective Practitioner: How Professionals Think in Action.* New York: Basic Books.

Scottish Government (2010) *Curriculum for Excellence Building the Curriculum 2 – Active Learning: A Guide to Developing Professional Practice.* Glasgow: Booksource.

Sheehy, N. (2004) *Fifty Key Thinkers in Psychology.* London: Routledge.

Siegler, R., DeLoache, J. and Eisenberg, N. (2010) (3rd Ed.) *How Children Develop.* New York: Worth.

Sing and Sign (2013) *The Benefits of Signing with your Baby are Potentially Significant.* Available from: http://www.singandsign.com/baby-signing/benefits-of-baby-signing (last accessed on 7 October 2013).

Siraj-Blatchford, I., Sylva, K., Muttock, S., Gilden, R. and Bell, D. (2002) *Researching the Effective Pedagogy in the Early Years.* Nottingham: DfES Publications.

Siraj-Blatchford, I. (2005) *Quality Interactions in the Early Years*. TACTYC Annual Conference: Birth to Eight Matters! Seeking Seamlessness – Continuity? Integration? Creativity? 5 November 2005, Cardiff.

Siraj-Blatchford, I. (2007) 'Creativity, Communication and Collaboration: the Identification of Pedagogic Progression in Sustained Shared Thinking'. *Asia-Pacific Journal of Research in Early Childhood Education*, Vol. 1, No. 2.

Siraj-Blatchford I. (2009) 'Conceptualising Progression in the Pedagogy of Play and Sustained Shared Thinking in Early Childhood Education: a Vygotskian perspective'. *Educational and Child Psychology*, Vol. 26, No. 2.

Skolverket (2010) *Curriculum for the Pre-school Lpfö 98 Revised 2010*. Stockholm: Fritzes kundservice. Available from http://www.skolverket.se/publikationer?id=2687 (last accessed 13 January 2014).

Skolverket (2011) *Curriculum for the Compulsory School, Pre-school Class and the Leisure-time Centre*. Stockholm: Skolverket Publications.

Stewart, N. (2011) *How Children Learn: The Characteristics of Effective Learning*. London: Early Education.

Stiera, J., Tryggvasonb, M., Sandströmc, M. and Sandbergd, A. (2012) 'Diversity Management in Pre-schools using a Critical Incident Approach'. *Intercultural Education* Vol. 23, Iss. 4, pp. 285–296.

Stone, S. and Stone, W. (2007) *Symbolic Play and Emergent Literacy*. Conference paper from the International Council for Children's Play Conference, Brno. Available from: http://www.iccp-play.org/documents/brno/stone1.pdf (last accessed on 13 October 2013).

Swedish Facts Figures and Publications: http://www.skolverket.se/om-skolverket/andra-sprak-och-lattlast/in-english.

Swedish Institute (2012) *Education in Sweden*. Available from: http://www.sweden.se/eng/Home/Education/Basic-education/Facts/Education-in-Sweden (last accessed on 30 June 2013).

Sylva, K., Melhuish, E., Sammons, P., Siraj-Blatchford, I. and Taggart, B. (2004) 'The Effective Provision of Pre-School Education [EPPE] Project': *Technical Paper 12 – The Final Report: Effective Pre-School Education*. A Longitudinal Study funded by the DfES 1997–2004. London: DfES.

Sylva, K., Melhuish, E., Sammons, P., Siraj-Blatchford, I. and Taggart, B. (2010) *Early Childhood Matters*. London: Routledge.

Teaching Agency (2013) *Early Years Professional Status Standards*. Available online at https://www.gov.uk/government/publications/early-years-teachers-standards (last accessed on 22 September 2013).

Tekin, A. (2011) 'Parents' Motivational Beliefs about their Involvement in Young Children's Education'. *Early Child Development and Care* Vol. 181, Iss. 10, pp. 1315–1329.

Theodorou, F. and Nind, M. (2010) 'Inclusion in Play: A Case Study of a Child with Autism in an Inclusive Nursery'. *Journal of Research in Special Educational Needs*, Vol. 10, No. 2, pp. 99–106.

Tickell, C. (2011) *The Early Years: Foundations for Life, Health and Learning*. London: DfE.

Trevarthen, C. (2011) 'What is it Like to be a Person who Knows Nothing? Defining the Active Intersubjective Mind of a Newborn Human Being'. *Infant and Child Development* Vol. 20 (Special Issue: *The Intersubjective Newborn*), Iss. 1, pp. 119–135.

United Nations Educational, Scientific and Cultural Organization (UNESCO) (2013) *Literacy Policy*. Available at: www.unesco.org/new/en/education/themes/education-building-blocks/literacy (last accessed on 26 October 2013).

University of Sheffield (2013) *A Framework for Early Literacy Development with Parents*. Available from http://www.real-online.group.shef.ac.uk/framework.html (last accessed on 4 August 2013).

Veale, F. (2013) 'The Early Years' Curriculum and Pedagogical Strategies to Support Learning and Development for Children' in Veale, F. *Early Years for Level 4 & 5 and the Foundation Degree*. Abingdon: Hodder Education.

Vygotsky, L. (1978) *Mind in Society*. Cambridge, MA: Harvard University Press.

Wagoner, B. (2011) 'Meaning Construction in Remembering: A Synthesis of Bartlett and Vygotsky' in: Stenner, J., Cromby, J., Motzkau, J., Yen, J. and Haosheng, Y. (Eds), *Theoretical Psychology: Global Transformations and Challenges* (pp. 105–114). Toronto: Captus Press.

Wall, K. (2011) *Special Needs and Early Years*. London: Sage.

Waterfield, R. (1992) *Essays by Plutarch on Listening*. London: Penguin Classics.

Weston, P. (2000) *Friedrich Froebel. His Life, Times and Significance*. London: Roehampton Institute.

Whalley, M. and Arnold, C. (2013) *Working with Families in Children's Centres and Early Years Settings*. London: Hodder Education.

White, J. (2002) *The Child's Mind*. London: Routledge Farmer.

Whitebread, D., Basilio, M., Kuvalja, M. and Verma, M. (2012) *The Importance of Play: A Report on the Value of Children's Play with a Series of Policy Recommendations*. Brussels, Belgium: Toys Industries for Europe.

Williams, P. (2008) *Independent Review of Mathematics Teaching in Early Years Settings and Primary Schools Final Report*. Nottingham: DCSF Publications.

Zussman, T. (2012) *Challenging Cultural Values that Affect Food Security in India*. Available from: http://www.eldis.org/go/topics/insights/2012/innovative-approaches-to-gender-and-food-security/challenging-cultural-values-that-affect-food-security-in-india#.Ul70sSh8zzI (last accessed on 16 October 2013).

Index

Printed in Great Britain
by Amazon